l
l
ë
3
Pl

2

- 8

--

Sul(l)

JULIA MARTIN

A Millimetre of Dust
Visiting Ancestral Sites

KWELA BOOKS

ALSO BY THE AUTHOR:

Writing Home (Carapace, 2002)

Some chapters from this book originally appeared, in a slightly
different form, in the following publications:
"Pattern", *The English Academy Review,* 22 (Dec 2005);
"The Kuruman Spring", *Social Dynamics*, 32: 2 (Dec 2006);
"Springbok, Farmers, Places and Shards: Reading and Writing the Bleek-Lloyd Archive",
Current Writing 19: 1 (2007)
and "Wonderwerk", *Maps of Reconciliation: Literature and the Ethical Imagination,*
a special issue of *Manoa* 19: 2 (2007).

Kwela Books,
an imprint of NB Publishers,
40 Heerengracht, Cape Town, South Africa
PO Box 6525, Roggebaai, 8012, South Africa
http://www.kwela.com

Cover design by swissarmy
Typography by Nazli Jacobs
Set in Palatino
Printed and bound by Paarl Print,
Oosterland Street, Paarl, South Africa

First edition, first impression 2008

ISBN-10: 0-7957-0263-9
ISBN-13: 978-0-7957-02631

for Gary Snyder

and all our relations

So the question I have been asking myself is: what says "humans"? What sucks *our* lineage into form? It is surely the "mountains and rivers without end" – the whole of this earth on which we find ourselves more or less competently at home.

GARY SNYDER

From the earliest times, human civilisation has been no more than a strange luminescence growing more intense by the hour, of which no one can say when it will begin to wane and when it will fade away. For the time being, our cities still shine through the night, and the fires still spread.

WG SEBALD

CONTENTS

Excavation   11

Archive   25

Travelling   44

Diamonds   63

Museum   77

Human   96

Animals   108

Pattern   125

Handaxes   139

Flamingos   146

Archaeologist   150

Treasures   159

Wonderwerk   163

Spring   184

Bodies   197

Impala   214

Ironstone   216

Stars   231

Home   243

Hearth   250

Sources   257

Acknowledgments   268

EXCAVATION

The bones were wet and soft. Already the head had collapsed, owing to the weight of the deposits above. It was nine feet down and the bone tools and implements were quite decomposed. The only things that remained intact were the indestructible stone artefacts and the common flakes.

So Bertie Peers described the excavation of a burial at Skildergat, or Peers' Cave, which he and his father undertook in the 1920s, a digging up of hidden things, of mutable, decaying things, forgotten things whose form falls into dust on exposure to the air, and things that hold the trace of transient generations, stone things that endure.

Victor Peers, an enthusiastic amateur botanist with an interest in natural history, had first explored the big cave up above the Fish Hoek dunelands while looking for plants. Born of a Welsh mining family, he came from Australia to South Africa to fight for the Commonwealth in what he would have called the Boer War. After being wounded in battle, Peers was so taken with the Cape flora he found on his walks that he went home to his sweetheart, Bella, determined to return. Once the couple had been married in Tasmania, they travelled to Cape Town to live in Wynberg. Victor got a job with the South African Railways, and they bought a house in Fish Hoek.

The excavation began in 1926. Whereas for many years archaeology in South Africa was to involve unnamed black workers doing much of the digging, this time it was different, a family affair. Every weekend Victor and his son, Bertie, worked together in the cave, as well as each day of their annual leave. In summer they were up there every evening, and Mrs Peers and their daughter, Dulcie, often lent a hand. They detonated, dug and sieved, and documented their work as well as they knew how. Photographs show Victor up at the site, staring unsmilingly at the camera, or father and son digging in the dust: strong, muscled men in shorts, wielding big spades and a large railway stoker's fork with ten long tines. In other pictures that call to mind many similar images of intelligent men looking at artefacts, Bertie is shown examining a find for the viewer to observe, a handsome man with a straight nose, his dark hair pushed back from a wide forehead. He wears a jacket with a white shirt, unbuttoned casually at the collar, his attention drawn to the piece of bone that he has unearthed.

Most of what they excavated consisted of thousands of stone artefacts of varying antiquity. But in the text of a slide lecture on "Ancient Fish Hoek Man and his Home" given in 1928 to the Natural History Club, Bertie concentrated on stories of the human remains that they had found.

Three bodies, he said, showed death by violence. Another must have had his life ended by misadventure, when the slab of rock immediately above his scattered bones caused his death. Another was laid to rest with only half a head, no spinal column, one and a half legs and one arm, and buried with one of the most perfect spearheads resting on the bones at the base of the skull.

At a depth of five feet they found the tiny bones of a baby, wrapped in a soft buckskin and placed on a bed of leaves. Bertie said the deposit was embedded in a hard layer of calcareous matter, a sort of lime carbonate acting as a preservative, which he thought had been caused by the heat of the fires a little way above. Carefully bundled and resting in leaves, the tiny child was buried with three strings of ostrich eggshell beads around the neck and a string of *Conus* shells for a rattle. He recorded that they had picked up the whole ball carefully and packed it in wadding.

In another part of the cave they found the fine skeleton of a young woman. Her wisdom teeth were just mature, he said, and her limbs and waist were garlanded with thousands of ostrich eggshell beads. A sort of beaded tiara arrangement rested below the knees in a beautifully worked pattern. The tiara was made of two kinds of beads, ostrich eggshell discs and wooden beads, which fitted together like a ball and socket: strings and strings of them fitted together, wooden beads impregnated with a crystalline substance which caused them to pulverise on exposure to air.

Around the young woman's neck and shoulders was another necklace from which hung nine prepared skin bags, sausage-shaped, as he described them, with carefully pleated ends, sewn up and strung on a thick twist of animal sinew at equal distances from each other. When they opened the bags, the men found water-smooth pieces of white quartz and the small leaves of an unnamed shrub.

Beside her head were three pieces of yellow ochre and two of bright red ochre, heavily scratched. A flake stone knife rested near them, which he believed would have been used for scraping the ochre into a powder before rubbing it into the body with a smooth body stone. Other tools buried with her were two water-worn pebbles that had been used as hammers and what he called a rare example of a long chipping stone. Her bones, he said, bore traces of ochre, and between her beads in their thousands they found the same traces again, markings of yellow and red, first pigments of our human kind.

As I read these words nearly eighty years later, the burial of this young woman – with herbs, tools and leather bags beneath the home cave floor, her body garlanded with beads and stories – seemed to me a gathering of all that is precious. Yet for Bertie and his father the excavation of Skildergat served rather to shed light on a people who were markedly different from themselves. Having used their findings to reflect on the curious customs, beliefs and extremely primitive arts and crafts of a race of ancient little men, Bertie felt able to say to the meeting of natural historians that, other than the quest for food, primitive man had little outlook in life. He was a born hunter, he told them, small of stature, with deep, sparkling eyes that missed nothing and a rather haggard expression on his drawn face. His body was rubbed with red or yellow ochre mixed with fat, which gave him a ferocious appearance, while around his arms, legs, waist and neck he wore strings of beads and other pendants of shell or bone.

Bertie believed that the same original stock of people once lived in sole possession of the country. But he considered their descendants, the remnants of the later races found here by the early European settlers, to have been doomed by their own natures. He explained to his audience, members of the Natural History Club, that civilised advancement and their peculiar temperaments could not permit the survival along with European settlers of the people he called the San. Unfortunately, it appeared that their wild ways would not allow domestication, for they did not know the meaning of "yours" and "mine". As a result, he said, they had to go, to make room for more honest men.[1]

This is not how most people who write about the past would interpret things today. But Bertie's view of the indigenous Khoe-San has a long history, which reaches back to the earliest European narratives about Southern Africa, and has continued in various forms well after his time.[2] Now awkward in the face of an earlier generation's prejudice, the guide at the Fish Hoek Valley Museum seemed apologetic when I asked her about the excavation. She said there were discrepancies between the different reports of their findings, and that not enough material had been retained for the excavation of the site to have much value for modern archaeology.

I came upon the story of Victor and Bertie Peers because of a mark engraved in the sandstone floor of an old Cape building. The place is called Het Posthuys, an early Dutch lookout post or tollhouse in Muizenberg, overlooking False Bay. The building is a small stone structure, not far from the thatched cottage where, on a narrow bed with a white lace coverlet, that definitive imperialist Cecil John Rhodes lay dying some generations later, with a view of the sea. Its actual date of origin is uncertain, but it is sometimes described as the oldest colonial house in the country, and is now a little museum. In one of the rooms the Battle of Muizenberg is depicted in a miniature diorama, which presents behind glass a blue False Bay, some sculpted mountains and one or two buildings. Numerous tiny soldiers are scattered across the painted green land in diverse poses, with redcoats advancing and blue Dutchmen defending. The guide tells you that the British ships each had sixty or seventy cannons on board and that in half an hour they fired eight hundred cannonballs. She gives you a cannonball to hold. It is heavy. Two hundred years later people are still picking them up on the mountain.

At the time I visited Het Posthuys I was writing about the False Bay coastline where my family lives, particularly about the shifting intertidal zone at the edge between land and sea. I had seen the teeming wild communities of seaweeds, mussels and anemones, but I also wanted to know more about the human cultures that came to inhabit the shore. When I asked the guide about who had lived in our neighbourhood before colonial occupation, she showed me a boat-shaped groove about the size of my hand in one of the floor stones. She explained that a few years ago, when the place was being renovated, someone had found the worked slab of sandstone nearby and it had been decided to set it into the floor. She said the people who had left it behind had probably used it for grinding ochre.

There are moments in one's life when things suddenly become clear or new. For me that morning, the quiet mark of human work in the sandstone floor was something extraordinary. Forgotten, left behind before the building of the first foundation, the stone was a tool for grinding, perhaps for grinding ochre. The stone was worked and used by people who lived where I now live. When I saw it for the first time in that small building peopled with colonial battles, the boat-shaped groove became for me a kind of sign, a trace of what was here before.

The guide was quite vague when I asked her for more information, but she sent me on to the Fish Hoek Valley Museum. Later that morning I found the place, a small suburban house near the library and civic centre, staffed by volunteers, with one room devoted to the story of Early Man in the region. In what must once have been someone's bedroom, the stone tools now lie in glass cases along the walls, classified according to a system established in South Africa in the 1920s. The sequence begins with the big, heavy symmetrical almond forms of the Earlier Stone Age handaxes. Then come the smaller Middle Stone Age points, blades, scrapers, flakes, cores. Then the fine, tiny artefacts of the Later Stone Age: quartz flakes, ostrich eggshell beads, tiny blades and scrapers.

I learnt that the same design of weighty handaxes and cleavers continued to be used across most of the so-called Old World for at least a million years. Then, gradually, in the later years, the tools for foraging and hunting were made to be smaller and smaller, until the set of worked stones a man or a woman used might fit into a leather bag, eland skin perhaps, carried over the shoulder, or around the waist, or hung from wooden pegs in a rock shelter. That was the last of it, here at least, before the guns and the machines. Yet a few strange liminal things remain, like a piece of imported flint, for instance, probably gun flint, that holds the marks of a worked-off edge.

The Stone Age exhibit is a collection of tools from the neighbourhood, donated by Dr EE Mossop. He was one of the original property owners in Fish Hoek, a place where I'm told that when the first plots were sold in 1918 a clause in the title deeds required that the property be sold only to people of the white race. Like Bertie and Victor Peers and others of their generation, Mossop was what is now called, with some disapproval on the part of professional archaeologists, an enthusiastic amateur. He was a medical doctor and a keen collector, and he kept the artefacts he found in stocking boxes. The contents were listed on the lids in a fine black Edwardian hand, and each lid was then varnished and the boxes stacked in order.

Now the tools rest in a small museum room beside an educational chart depicting the changing coastline of the region through long ice ages and the warmer years between. The chart shows that there were times, long times, when the mountains where we live now were islands in the sea. Later, as the waters began to recede, as recently as eighteen thousand years ago, False Bay became a sandy plain inhabited by people and other animals. Then, as the earth warmed and the polar icecaps thawed, the sea rose again. The coast retreated inland, and the territory became a realm of lakes and vleis.

On the walls are copies of Bertie Peers's watercolours of the patterns of dots and grids that they found on the rock surface of the cave. The guide told me that they are probably what are called entoptics – patterns recording the imagery of altered states of mind, memories of the trance. She said that Victor and Bertie's most celebrated discovery, what they called Fish Hoek Man, was a 12 000-year-old skull, which in its heyday travelled all around the archaeological world and now resides at the Iziko South African Museum in Cape Town, along with some of the bones and artefacts from the cave, their labels eaten by mice. Since the days of their enthusiasm, she said, the paintings have been vandalised and effaced, and all that remains of the work of their weekend shovels is an empty cave which bears the family name.

Yet stone tools from the region still rest under glass, organised and labelled in Mossop's hand. Five hundred thousand years old, maybe a million or more, the symmetry of the oldest artefacts endures through all the changes of land and sea. They came from here, the place where we now live, here where archaeological divers may still find stone artefacts at the bottom of False Bay. This is where they lived, people and animals. This is where the tools were used. Cemented into the floor of the old Dutch lookout post is a boat-shaped groove in the stone: forgotten, left behind, this trace of the women and men and children who were here before.

I came home to the tall house built in 1929, around the time of the Peers excavation, and perceived for the first time our neighbourhood of mountain, coastline, valley, dunelands, inhabited for hundreds of thousands of years.

It was early winter, that first winter when rain did not fall. The garden was very dry, and every day the cloudless sky was blue. For the first time everyone I knew was worried.

Hearing about the European summer in which people were dying from heat exhaustion and the forests were on fire, I remembered WG Sebald's idea that all human culture is founded on burning. In *The Rings of Saturn*, some years before the crisis of global climate change or the concept of a carbon footprint had become a regular priority in the international media, he considered the destruction of the dense forests that extended over the British Isles after the last ice age. From the beginning, he wrote, it has all been combustion. Combustion is the hidden principle behind every new artefact we create. For the spread of human civilisation over the earth was fuelled by reducing the higher species of vegetation to charcoal, by incessantly burning whatever would burn.[3]

That winter in Cape Town became for me then the image of a parched civilisation that is burning itself up with an insatiable desire. On the news, predictions of climate change saw the entire western half of South Africa becoming an uninhabitable desert within fifty years, within the lifetime of people who are now children.

In retrospect, this accumulation of disquiet that the unseasonable weather had provoked could be the reason why my visit to the little museums that morning seemed so welcome, and why the quiet mark in the sandstone floor and the worked stone tools that Mossop had collected came to resemble something precious as water, a memory that is almost forgotten. Call it nostalgia, avoidance, or sentimentality, perhaps. But, like others who have looked to their forebears for guidance in times of distress, it seemed to me then that the long long years before all this, before even the technologies of livestock and cultivated fields, might hold some trace of that which has been lost, and that which we might yet remember.

Wanting to see the Peers collection and to learn more about its story, I visited the Iziko South African Museum to meet with Royden Yates, an archaeologist who had researched Peers' Cave in recent years.

The museum is situated in the heart of the Mother City, where oak trees, pears and roses retain some memory of that first garden planted on this site, as I was told at school, for the innocent cultivation of fresh fruit and vegetables. There were big cats in Cape Town in those days, and hippos that lived behind the fort. Van Riebeeck recorded in 1653 that lions had stormed the walls for the sheep within, and noted that they roared horribly. It is said that black rhino still lived on the Cape Flats at that time and on the slopes of Table Mountain, and that the last elephant was shot only in 1702. It is said that by the middle of the eighteenth century, the kudu, eland and red hartebeest that he describes in his journal had all been exterminated from the immediate vicinity, though hyenas still scavenged the streets around the slaughterhouses.

I learnt about these animals from an ageing notice board outside the museum's natural history collection of stuffed animals. From a more recent generation of visitors' information, I read that the word "iziko" means hearth. I understand that at the excavation of an archaeological site the accumulation of burnt bones, worked stones, ostrich eggshells, bulbs and other things that may constitute a hearth is usually a crucial record of habitation.

Over coffee in his office, Royden explained that nowadays people tend to associate the chaos of the Peers' Cave collection with Victor and Bertie's methods of excavation. Father and son are generally seen as amateurs trashing the cave, whereas real scientists would have gone about things differently. But in fact, he said, their approach was not that different from the way professionals were working at the time. And Bertie Peers was in communication with the first professional archaeologist in the country, John Goodwin, who was influential in defining the frameworks that shaped the discipline in the years to come.

"Goodwin's standard of excavation was better," Royden said, "but not hugely so. The main difference was that Bertie didn't use a grid. But he was astute, really bright. Of course, he didn't look after the stuff properly."

We took the lift up to the storeroom to see the collection. The room was lined with tall metal shelves on which were stacked hundreds of large brown cardboard boxes. At the Peers' Cave section we found boxes heavy with excavated things and opened them at random, holding the artefacts in our hands. In one there was a packet with pieces of red ochre, and a collection of Middle Stone Age tools. Another box held hammerstones and grinding stones, one still marked with red ochre. In a third was a slender white clay pipe, broken at several points and stamped on the bowl with a British crown. As to depth or origin, some of the labels on the boxes indicated more or less where things had been found, but others recorded only uncertainty.

"Do you know where the burials are?" I asked, thinking of the baby wrapped in buckskin, and the young woman garlanded with beads.

"They're somewhere here, but where precisely I don't know. I've never seen the buckskin, though, or the leather bags. Must have been removed along the way."

Removed, displaced, unprovenanced. The assembled things in cardboard boxes seemed to me empty of sign or memory, quiet and lost as the leavings of some recent destruction.

In the days that followed, these placeless artefacts accompanied my thoughts, along with the image of the boat-shaped groove in the sandstone floor, which remained quite clear and evocative. Then one day I remembered with a sort of yearning the story of a different thing, a place in the heart of the land where the Early Stone Age handaxes still lie in their multitudes a metre deep. The story seemed fantastical, some traveller's tale of a great wide field of worked-off stones, a land of stone artefacts impossibly vast and old, a dream of lithic things enduring beyond and before the narratives of history, a forgotten wonder somewhere in the dry regions of the Northern Cape.

I called our friend the archaeologist, Duncan Miller, who had first described it to me, and he said that the place was a site named Kathu Townlands and that it was near Kuruman.

"It's really vast," he said, "several rugby fields, as far as you can see."

Irresistibly, I wanted now to see.

ARCHIVE

O nce having made the decision to visit the Northern Cape, I began to read about Kathu and also about other Stone Age sites in the area – places with names like Canteen Kopje and Driekopseiland and Wonderwerk Cave. I found that the meticulous records of stratigraphy and sedimentology at these sites, of pebbles and different-coloured sands, of lithic artefacts and faunal remains, of engravings and paintings, of pollens and grasses, were to offer a kind of refuge in the distress of that dry winter. The care and precision of the unfamiliar scientific words was strangely soothing, whatever the excavations which had produced them.

At the same time a more narrative impulse meant that I was also interested in story and metaphor, and in hearing about the region from other voices. For this I turned, like many others in recent years, to the Bleek-Lloyd Archive of /Xam testimonies recorded in the late nineteenth century in a collection of notebooks. Here I found a multitude of images and stories. These led me to the work of others who had also studied them, and then to one last story in particular.

In the Manuscripts and Archives Library at the University of Cape Town my work for the day consists of sitting on a chair at a table and reading stories told by members of a hunting and gathering people whose culture was exterminated by modern ones.

Catalogued here as the Bleek Collection, the archive is an assembly of more than eleven thousand notebook pages of script, which records and translates into English the testimonies of a group of /Xam-speaking San. The project was initiated in 1866 by the philologist Dr Wilhelm Bleek, who was soon joined in the recording process by his sister-in-law Lucy Lloyd. After his death, she carried on with the work until around 1884.

Among their informants were //Kabbo and his son-in-law /Han≠kass'o, Dia!kwain, his sister !Kweiten-ta-//ken and her husband, ≠Kasin, and also /A!kunta. The men were prisoners at the Breakwater Prison in Cape Town who had been serving sentences for offences ranging from stock theft to culpable homicide in the part of the country which was then called Bushmanland. They lived in the Bleek household in Mowbray at different times, sometimes with members of their families, in order for Bleek and Lloyd to record their language and stories.

While Bertie and Victor Peers may have conceived of the people whose remains they excavated as being less than fully human, the forty years older Bleek-Lloyd Archive embodies a more sympathetic and complex view on the part of the researchers. Like his Victorian contemporaries in other fields, Wilhelm Bleek was certainly drawn to the practices of collection, classification and measurement as a definitive means of understanding the world and, in this case, indigenous people. But while the recording process may have begun as an investigation of the informants as specimens of a type, or as objects of study, his attitude towards the people who became part of his household evolved over the years into something more humane than this would suggest. For their part, the Bushman informants (as they were called) seem to have been willing, often eager, for their stories to be written down, some of them travelling all the way back from the Northern Cape to Mowbray simply to continue with the project. This extended and serious commitment on the part of both researchers and informants to the recording process was something extraordinary and probably unprecedented.

By the late twentieth century, within a generation or so of the Peers excavation, the archive had become very influential in the interpretation of rock art in South Africa and further afield, and its stories an unparalleled source for contemporary people wishing to imagine the cultures of Khoe-San or San or /Xam, or hunting and gathering.

Such late modern imaginings are possibly as ideologically laden and full of fear and longing as was the Peers' account of ancient little men. Translation and interpretation are always in a sense betrayal, and particularly so in this case, when the fragments of /Xam are written into a Victorian English, the stories of animals and people are read from our contemporary frame, a particular group of informants are made to become the representative voice of a whole way of life, and the whole collection a record of practices and attitudes on the brink of extinction.

Inevitably, then, as with other visitors to the archive, or travellers who tell the tale of a journey, my reading is also a kind of reconstruction.

Across the room from my table in the Manuscripts and Archives Library two German researchers are working on a fat folder of documents from the Struggle Era. Behind me fingers click fast on a laptop like mine, while at another of the tables, studying what he tells me are letters that he has discovered from Jemima Bleek to her husband Wilhelm, is one of my colleagues, the historian Andrew Bank, who is working on a book about the collection.[4] The small room is quiet, polished, serious, clean, and the artefacts we are investigating are texts, maps and pictures, not stones or grubby bits of bone. Though we're each equipped with certain tools and expectations, unlike Bertie and his father, we do not need to alter the record of the past irrevocably in order to do this research, and the conditions for metaphorically excavating information seem really as congenial as one could hope for.

The librarian smiles considerately as she places four marbled hardcover exercise books on my table. I savour the simple touch of one of them in my hands. I had not anticipated the beautiful materiality of the notebooks that make up the collection, one hundred and fifty-eight of them in all, with covers made of rippled pools and swirls, the random watery pattern of coloured inks, green marbling, brown and blue, red and black, red and gold, or plain pale fawn or brown, each small book distinct and labelled. Sitting at ease in the comfortable room, I hold one of Lucy Lloyd's notebooks dated 1878, feel its weight, and imagine the succession of hands through which this ripple-marbled book has passed. It must have been held in the hands of the people who made the paper and those who bound it, in the hands of a salesman, perhaps, and a shopkeeper, in Lucy's 44-year-old hands, holding the notebook when it was new and bright, and holding the fountain pen with which she wrote. Later it was held in the hands of Dorothea Bleek, Wilhelm's daughter, who made the collection more widely available, and in the hands of readers and writers and librarians and researchers.

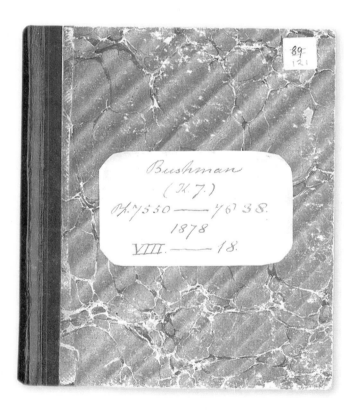

Now the exercise book rests in my own hands, a curious artefact of contact. The rippled pattern on the cover is a flowing stream of red,

red as blood, red as the blood of an eland, red as the blood of the Bosjemans the settlers hunted down, faded now and worn from the touch of many hands. The right-hand page of the book is divided into two columns, one for the /Xam and the other for the English translation. Two languages face each other, their words transcribed in ink in a lively hand. I wonder whether the informants, /A!kunta, Dia!kwain, //Kabbo, /Han≠kass'o, !Kweiten-ta-//ken or ≠Kasin, ever held in their hands these notebooks in which their stories were recorded.

But beyond the sensual touch of this material thing, what can I learn from its words? I might wish them to be the voices of a Stone Age world speaking its truth to a colonial ear, or even to a modern globalised one like mine. But I know that they must be something more particular, more complexly inflected. The archive cannot be transparent, cannot be a window through which to see a people called Khoe-San or San or even /Xam. Instead, the glass, to follow a metaphor, must always be somewhat scratched and clouded, reflective and misted in parts and sometimes broken, a gathering of shards and fragments, like the basket of smashed china we keep at home to use one day for making a mosaic. Before this visit to the archive, I read the stories and poems that other people have extracted from the collection, bits gathered and cemented together to make up an ethnography, a history, poetry, art. Now that the original notebooks are on the desk before me, I can see that their appeal seems almost irresistible. On every page a so-called found poem could appear to gleam, fragrant with image and allusion.

In a notebook labelled *Bushman M.S. pp 1-333 1866-1871*, the collection begins with a record of words and phrases given to Wilhelm Bleek by Adam Kleinhardt at the Breakwater Prison before the project began in earnest or any of the informants went to live in the Mowbray house. Here at the beginning, writing down first words, writing down a language, trying to understand, these are the words on page one, the words translated into English:

> ribs;
>
> heart of ox;
>
> thy heart;
>
> my heart is sore;
>
> ox lungs;
>
> ox lung;
>
> my lungs are sore;
>
> ox liver;
>
> my liver is sore;
>
> the Bushmen eat the cattle of the Boers;
>
> the Boers take the children of the Bushmen.[5]

The words are simple, stark. I wonder how the utterance of these particular words was initiated, how Adam Kleinhardt chose to begin with this story of pain.

Reading on, I notice that in this bare beginning and in the testimonies that follow, each page bears witness to a fine attention to the detail of experience, both on the part of the informants and in the work of those who were writing it down. Whatever diverse attitudes, styles and personal histories Bleek and Lloyd and each of the informants brought to the recording sessions, what is remembered in the notebooks are image, story, metaphor, the precise details of things, not abstract ideas.

So each day, after driving to the university in my car, I read about stones and arrows, about talking stars and talking flowers, stories of husbands, wives, fathers, mothers and grandparents, and cautionary tales for children. There are stories of hunting and the preparation of meat, stories of a time when animals were people and people were animals, stories about water and waterholes, rain and rain's things, and about the use of ochre and specularite. And running a track of blood through the notebooks are stories about farmers and Boers and commandos and cruelty and dispossession. In the pages I read, the telling tends to be repetitive, the syntax incantatory. The English translation is full of Biblical resonances and Victorian phrasing, and the word order sounds quaint in contemporary usage. Sometimes for pages only the /Xam column is filled in while the other side is left blank, save for the odd word that floats free: "child . . . old people . . . they understand . . . shoots . . . eat . . . heart". I wonder what else has been left out.

Again I need to remind myself that neither the /Xam stories nor their silences can really be Stone Age words speaking to the Age of Iron and Steel. Still, the recording project was a sustained and serious attempt to salvage traces of a way of life that was in the process of being extinguished. And the people who spoke these words could tell about things that humans had been doing for a million years or more: Stone Age things, hunting and gathering things, a thread of knowledge passing down the generations, a thread that seems for us now to have been broken.

As recently as 1873, ≠Kasin could describe to Lucy Lloyd how to make stone tools. Here is her account of it:

> Klaas says that the stone of which the Bushmen make //kutten //kutten is not to be found down here. They make little ones from white stones which they split, and make the split pieces into arrow-heads. There are large red stones from which they make arrow-heads and also knives. Some of the little stones are also red inside. Flints are, Klaas says, to be found at his place, at least stones such as two flints he shows me, which come from a stone he picked up by the sea – but the stone from which they make their //kutten //kutten is different.[6]

On another occasion, /Han≠kass'o told her, "Stones are those with which we skin . . . we skin the springbok with them," and went on to describe in detail how to make arrows.[7]

These words seem to me now both tantalisingly recent and irretrievable, stories of stones and the making of tools. Beside me the researchers of Manuscripts and Archives sit quietly, seriously at their tables.

They look like historians, and I expect they know what they are up to. Their confidence and industry make me nervous because I do not really understand what it is that I am doing here, or exactly what desires or even myths might have brought me to this place.

For Bertie Peers and his father the powerful myth of their own civilisation seems to have obscured from them the humanity of the people whose remains they excavated. For many people since, the stories in the Bleek-Lloyd Collection have seemed to confirm an almost opposite view of Khoe-San people.

Writing about this kind of interpretation, Andrew Bank has suggested that some readers have tended to believe that the /Xam informants were expressing a sustained connection with a realm of ungoverned nature that dwells beyond the walls of the colonial house.[8] According to this way of seeing, which Andrew has called the garden myth, Wilhelm Bleek and Lucy Lloyd would have been encountering through their contact with //Kabbo and the others a way of seeing and being that spoke of Eden before the Fall, a healing truth which we have forgotten. For industrialised people now facing global climate change and the pervasive crisis of environment and development, the idea is certainly a tempting one. But, of course, if we are sensible, we will remember that to think this way is, as they say, romanticised, nostalgic, a projection of otherness onto people who seem different from ourselves, a reflection of our longing and desire.

For other interpretations, you could look into the unique gathering of meandering narrative and focused attention that makes up the archive and discover a key to the reading of rock art, shamanism and the trance. You could trace the ambiguous record of a colonial encounter, or read a complex story of hunting and foraging, or of adaptation and survival in a harsh ecology. You could read the collection as evidence of the primitive lives of Bertie Peers's little men, or find in it a remarkable record of human stories from the late nineteenth century. You could discover lies or truth or poetry or art, pages written in a confident Victorian hand, or a gathering of gaps and fragments.

I wonder whether any of these metaphors of vision and discovery describe my purpose. Whatever else, the collection records a rare dialogue between people from very different environments, and it assembled a vast store of narratives from a few members of a remnant hunting and gathering people in the last years of their culture. They were people whose ancestors may have lived where my family now lives in Muizenberg, and in the dry Northern Cape, where I now mean to go. In part, then, I am simply hoping to find some words in this collection to accompany me on the journey, words that remember the last years of Stone Age technologies in the region and speak about places, animals, stars, rain, people, tools.

Beyond this, or probably before it, the desire that I bring to the archive is something more personal, an inclination that began with my father in the suburban landscape of apartheid Pietermaritzburg. He might have been reading Laurens van der Post, I don't know, but somehow during my childhood he came to believe that human beings should really be hunters and gatherers, with a nomadic relation to the land, minimal possessions and an egalitarian social structure. He felt keenly the tragedy of the loss of this imagined way of life, and used to say he was off hunting and gathering when going to the supermarket for family groceries. He was funny and playful when he said it, but I think in a sense he meant it, and that in a sense I believed him.

So when I read the marbled notebooks now, I probably carry with me an intention that began with my father's particular garden myth (although my sense of it has changed over the years). Having grown up with his form of social critique, his longing for another way, and all his books and stories and music, I think my understanding of this inheritance means that I would like to believe in the possibility of telling stories that are different from the powerful narratives of mastery, conquest and destruction that wielded authority in his own life and have come to dominate the world.

So, like all the other readers (and like the researchers and informants themselves), I bring questions to the archive that are full of projection and desire. In particular, I am interested in how the notebooks describe the relations between things and people. Or between selves and others. Or people and places. Paging through the heap of /Xam testimonies, I have hoped to meet a different way of seeing from that which the voices of late industrial civilisation seem to take for granted. Or ways of speaking about what it is to be a person or an animal, what it is to have a point of view, that could tell another story.

Looking for such things, I find in a notebook dated 1878 these words from /Han≠kass'o to Lucy Lloyd:

We who are Bushmen, were once springbucks, and the Mantis shot us, and we really cried (like a little child). Then the Mantis said, we should become a person, become people, because we really cried.[9]

A year later he told her what the springbok mothers sing when they are soothing their springbok children. Here are the words of their song, written in Lucy's hand amid a heap of notes, somewhere near the bottom of a page:

Oh! Springbok child!
Sleep for me!
Oh! Springbok child!
Sleep for me![10]

In a sense this is just what I have been after: people who were once springbok, springbok who were people, an idea of personhood that is more fluid and inclusive than my own. Once seen, I find it again and again.

Yet the more I read, the clearer it becomes that this particular idea is but a narrow track through a world of words that is both compendious and incomplete. The collection is a gathering of artefacts and fragments, a basket of shards, yet their pain and beauty and the extraordinary collective endeavour that they represent are unarguable. So too is the compelling immediacy of these words, and the sense that they communicate of inhabiting a living world. While there is no single thought by which to frame the meaning of this organised assemblage, one might try a metaphor to describe it: call the archive a kind of treasure, or a cache of dreams and nightmares, or an ark constructed to hold its creatures against the Flood, or simply sweet water stored in a time of drought.

After reading some of the /Xam testimonies I make an appointment to visit the archaeologist Janette Deacon. Like a number of other researchers, she has drawn on the Bleek-Lloyd material, but her specific interest has been to do with place or places: tracking through the notebooks for a sense of how the informants understood their relation to their environment, identifying how the places they called home were marked and mapped, and then locating and studying the actual neighbourhoods where they lived. In the process she became familiar with a particularly unvisited region of the Northern Cape and happened on another story.

The area is between Upington and Calvinia, identifiable by current place names like Kenhardt, Brandvlei, Vanwyksvlei. It is also known as /Xam-ka !au, the land of the /Xam, what the archive calls the Flat Bushman territory and the Grass Bushman territory, the driest part of the country, annexed to the Cape Colony under the name of Bushmanland in 1847. When I was a child, the voices of radio announcers reading the weather report after the news intoned the mysterious phrase with a particular upward inflection that I recall quite precisely:

"Bushmanland and the Karoo region". Raised as I was on dreams of a green and pleasant land, that cheerfully uttered name of an unknown place, where it was always hot and inhospitable, would have seemed to me then an unlikely destination. But now the idea of visiting the Northern Cape has come to possess me, and I am curious.

Janette has shown that the whole territory used to be intimately inhabited and the country peopled with stories. Each place was known and named, each pool and pan and watercourse, and the tall white grass that turns golden in the morning and evening light in a year of good rain. So there is //Kabbo's place, she writes, the Bitterpits, where the water tastes brackish. There is the pan where Dia!kwain, after burying his wife, saw a thing sitting that looked like a little child wearing the hat his wife used to wear. There is the place called /kann where Dia!kwain's father made chippings of animals on the rock. There is the mountain where the !khau lizard was broken in half so that his head and shoulders became one hill and his legs and tail became another. There is the Rooiberg where people collect ochre. There is the place where it is told that Smoke's Man saw the wind.[11]

But the particular story of this region that I have come to hear her tell is a more recent one about a man called Hendrik Goud whom she met on one of her field trips.

"He was a tall man," she says, "thin and probably about eighty years old at the time. He was working as a gardener at the farmhouse. When I saw him there, I suggested to the farmer that perhaps he might remember something. So we went over to talk to him."

Janette and I are drinking tea from floral-patterned porcelain cups in the sitting room of her Stellenbosch house, with a cat asleep on an armchair. Backtracking, she describes how, following the traces of names and stories in the narratives, she and her fellow researchers came in 1985 to the farm near Gifvlei called Katkop, a place that Dia!kwain considered to be his home.

"The farmer was really gracious and helpful," she says. "His name was Johannes Hendrikse. He was born in 1905. Although he worked as a teacher in Keimoes for part of his adult life, the farm was always home. I asked him whether he remembered anyone with the surname Hoesar – David Hoesar was, of course, Dia!kwain's colonial name.

"Oom Johannes said, yes, there was a boy he'd known on the farm since childhood called Klaas Hoesar, a 'wilde Boesman'. Then he pointed to the scar on his cheek and said it was from the time Klaas threw a stone at him when they were children. He said, 'Hy het my met 'n klip gegooi.'"

Now Klaas himself was long gone, and it seemed from what the farmer could tell that there was nobody left on the farm who might remember anything of the /Xam. Then Janette suggested they try speaking to the old gardener, who, she says, was clearly of San descent.

"We introduced ourselves, and he said his name was Hendrik Goud. At first, when the farmer asked him if he knew anything about the Bushman language, he said sorry, no, he didn't know anything. Then the next morning he came over to speak to me just before we left. It was about six-thirty and we were getting ready for an early start."

She pauses and smiles, remembering.

"The old man sort of sidled up to me and said, yes, there actually was something he remembered 'in die /Xam taal'. I thought it was quite significant that he used the term /Xam without our prompting. The farmer had said 'Boesman'."

It was a hundred years since Lucy Lloyd's last interviews, and when Hendrik Goud said he knew a few words in /Xam, he was probably the last person in the region to remember anything of the language. He spoke the words he knew and Janette got the tape recorder out of the car and recorded him. Afterwards they thanked him, finished packing the car and went on their way.

"It's one of the regrets of my life that I didn't take his photograph," she says ruefully, "but at least we taped the words."

They were not many words, barely two sentences. Hendrik spoke the /Xam words and then translated. What it meant, he said, was "Hier kom die Boere. Ons moet weghardloop."

The recording was later analysed by Tony Traill at Wits University, using a system derived from the Bleek-Lloyd material. Here the last /Xam words were interpreted to be /hu kwa koa se: /ke //a, and translated as "White man comes yonder, run". Or "Here come the Boere, we must run away". Or "Hier kom die Boere, ons moet weg-hardloop".

Janette explains that she generally uses "colonists" in favour of "whites", or in this case, because of Hendrik's understanding of the words, "farmers". She says it took someone with a good ear for San languages to distinguish what he had said, that although they were recognisable, his words seemed to have been eroded away from the original /Xam utterance, like a child's chant or spell that has been re-peated and repeated long after the meaning of the particular words has been forgotten.

I have read several accounts of this meeting in Janette's writings, but wanted to listen to her telling it as a story, to see the old man from her description. She gave me more than I had asked for – references, pictures, and the poignant companionship of people who own houses in the city and drive their cars to work and imagine through the gra-ciousness of tea and conversation the quality of other lives and places, and the horror of their destruction.

By the time my family and I set off for the Northern Cape, leaving behind our house and computers in Cape Town, the urgent concerns of reading and interpretation quickly become distant city words, words of the virtual world. Travelling through the land on a fast new road, I almost feel as though the chattering words might be dissolving in our wake, like smoke into the air.

Here they lived, here in this region. It was always a harsh environ-ment, and people did die of starvation. But after good rains, the grass grew high and golden, and the buck came galloping. This desert, they said, was peopled with animals and rain's things and human beings who knew their stories, people who were once springbok, springbok who were once people. The springbok mothers sang songs to soothe their children, and at those times when the great migrations came passing through, the herds of springbok were many.

As recently as 1878 /Han≠kass'o was recorded as saying that the springbok are so many that they resemble the water of the sea. The sea is no desert metaphor, but perhaps he had seen it from his cell in the Breakwater Prison, great waves rolling in like the springbok he remembered (or wished to remember) on the faraway plains of home, countless as longing. Continuing, he described how the springbok came in great numbers, and that the Boers' gunpowder became exhausted, that and the balls.[12]

A hundred years later when Janette visited the region, the multitudes of springbok were gone, the grass was cropped short by sheep and the old people had been destroyed. A hundred years after Adam Kleinhardt's first bare utterances had been listed in a notebook by Wilhelm Bleek, the only /Xam words left were "Here come the Boere. We must run away."

Run, here come the farmers. Here come the people from the city. Here we now come to the places where they lived, our heads full of stories and desire. Here we come driving through a wide, dry land, where the great waves of springbok have been almost forgotten, driving towards Kimberley, as it is called.

TRAVELLING

B efore the young tar road and the slow wagon journeys of discovery and occupation that claimed this route through the territory, the various land was marked with smaller paths and tracks, the pans and waterholes inscribed with other stories and the tread of many feet. Now, travelling through from Cape Town to Kimberley, dawn to dusk, the road is a long, fast bridge from here to there. The travelling eye becomes a little window, the land a landscape rushing by.

With my husband, Michael, driving and our young twins, Sophie and Sky, strapped into the back seats, the small car is cluttered with city things. Along with all this stuff, I cannot help imagining that we also carry with us the ambiguous inheritance of those imperial travellers from the Cape who took this way before, their wagons laden with collecting boxes, sketchbooks, guns and journals, equipment of their quest. Having left behind the comforts and conveniences of settled community, they named the plants and animals, documented the curious and primitive behaviour of other peoples and strove to establish the place and characteristics of every single discrete thing they found.

Was it their intention to promote the civilised business of prejudice and coercive power? Like Dr Mossop and the Peers family in Fish Hoek, such people were often enthusiastic amateurs, absorbed in the adventure of exploration and of natural science.[13]

Like certain of these predecessors, I hope that leaving the city for a while might clear the mind, that the open vastness of the desert might help me to remember what is real, to discover some treasure in the wild. But while the intrepid journeys of the early travellers were slow and dangerous, our family's passage through the territory now is fast and relatively comfortable. We are driving a 1300 Ford and are equipped with a Nokia cellphone and an HP digital camera. The car is packed with food and bags of clothes and shoes and an array of books and soft animals. The only real challenges on our trip are modern and domestic: the fact of two small children in the back seat, for example.

In the days before leaving home, Michael and I tell the twins repeatedly that they will not be allowed, not even once, to ask "Are we nearly there yet?" They are also not to fight or whine.

My mother's advice for such journeys is to keep everyone fed. So, as soon as we are out of Cape Town I give them each a banana, which they share with the large extended family of soft animals that is accompanying us. The bears, the dog, the owl and the rabbits are very excited about the journey. So are the children. Nearly six years old, they have never before travelled so far from home.

As we leave the house in Muizenberg just before dawn, the electric network of the city lies before us like a pattern of stars assembled in the dark. Our car joins the morning traffic, each vehicle a bright jewel burning the fossil fuel, a precious artefact of steel and engineering. Each shining light is linked to the others in a moving chain which threads a humming, jewelled garland across the city, driving onwards. Almost invisibly, the gases from our exhaust pipes dissolve in the cold air which is fresh as morning, luminous as dawn. In the direction of our particular journey, the mountains set a blue rim against the brightening day.

The sun comes up as we approach the Hex River Valley, a territory which is sometimes described as the threshold, the last bit of formal cultivation before Africa begins. But the patchwork grids of vineyards planted in neat, farmed rows of irrigated squares remind me, not of Europe, but of pictures in a book I once bought in a Chinese shop in London sometime in the 1980s. They are nearly all landscapes, cheerful prints depicting a region called Huhsien County, in which the land is ploughed, hoed, irrigated and planted with rice, cotton, wheat, persimmons, cabbages or peppers. Each scene illustrates an advance in the heroic struggle for Production and Scientific Experiment, as it is called. Each plain is made of rectangular fields. Each hill is terraced. In the ancient tradition of Chinese landscape art, people tend to appear as tiny figures on a great expanse, small selves inscribed in the pattern of something vast. But in the new dispensation everything has been reconstructed – the ancient rocks and waterfalls, the forests, and even the tall, wild mountains rising out of morning mist. In their place, the New Mountain Scene depicts canals, plantations and electricity, the land imprinted with the People's industrious power. The pictures are bright and joyous, sometimes beautiful.

Here in the Western Cape, the patterns of irrigated farmland are similar. But the last reach of mountain above the fields is still wild, and the system of ownership is obviously different. Beside the vineyards is the squatter camp, that seemingly inevitable companion of wealth in this country. From our car, passing through, we glimpse a neighbourhood of little houses made of tin and plastic, the roofs held down with stones, grey stones on the roof, and the ground between the shacks stripped bare of plants, stripped bare it seems of every colour except grey. Beyond these shacks and stones the cultivated rows and squares across the land recall the eye to colour and pattern. Each vine grows on a wooden support and the fabric of greens and reds and browns is pleasing in the early morning light. On the edge of the road, farm labourers stand holding out boxes of grapes to sell to the passing motorists. One man in particular leans back with his foot outstretched as though doing the cakewalk, his arm extended too in an ironic pose, proffering the last sweet grapes of the year as we roar past.

Between Laingsburg and Beaufort West the road is a long straight line through dry land, that part of the journey which people tell you is boring and uneventful, terra nullius, empty of interest. Signs tell drivers to rest if tired, and there are bumps on the tar to wake you up or slow you down. For lunch, we stop to eat sandwiches at a concrete picnic table on the side of the road. Sophie climbs up to balance on one of the concrete chairs, then leaps to the next one and misses, falling hard with her chest against the edge of the slab. Crying, crying, she says it's really sore. I hold her close, but not too tight. For weeks the small cracked rib aches.

As the hours pass we hand out juice and chocolate digestive biscuits, play I Spy for a while, and listen to funny English rhymes and the unpleasant story of Hansel and Gretel on Granny's portable tape recorder. When the sun begins to shine directly into the car, the twins' blue eyes and milky pale skins need protection, so I trap a flapping T-shirt in the window to make a sort of screen and put on hats and sunblock as they wriggle away from my smeary hands, afraid of stinging eyes. Instead of asking are we nearly there yet, the children want to know how many hours we have been travelling. We have told them that it is about ten to Kimberley, so this is a way of finding their bearings in the endless space of the day. At intervals we talk about what the others must be doing at kindergarten in Cape Town. Circle time, break time, playtime, home time. When someone needs immediately to wee, we stop at the side of the road and walk out into the prickly grass, feet humming still with the movement of the car. At once the scrub is alive with grasshoppers, ants, tiny flowers and butterflies. Stop, breathe, look around. Still, the day is hot and we want to get going.

Driving on, the grey of the squatter camp appears again in the battery chicken factories beside the road, grey concentration camps planted among green kikuyu lawns. In the small towns we recognise the city shops – Truworths, Shoprite, Foschini, Mr Price, OK, Sheet Street. At Leeu Gamka hundreds of dusty ostriches pace anxiously about in small enclosures, the fenced ground stripped of any plant, just the ostriches pacing among pale grey stones and dust.

From Three Sisters the landscape is described as becoming more beautiful. The sheep-eaten scrub, the koppie, the rim of blue mountains on the horizon, the windmill, the golden poplars, the tiny railway station and the farmhouse look like the setting for a plaasroman, some story of drought and dust, of race and labour and blood and inheritance, of veld grass, gumtrees, dongas, and lands where no crop will grow.

There is a description of just such a farm in the feisty journal of one Mary Elizabeth Barber, who took a wagon journey through the region in 1879 at the age of sixty-one:

> Over the flats for many miles we travelled, and at length rested our weary cattle, by spanning out near a boer's homestead, where, close to the dwelling house, was the usual kraal and Kafir huts, the small dam, and weak attempt at making a garden, which consisted of two or three willow trees, a few miserable American aloes (*Agave americana*), a broken down fig tree, a couple of lonely, melancholy-looking Blue Gums.[14]

Mary Barber was, of course, a woman, though a rather unusual one for her time. Since her twenties she had been fascinated by botany, an interest which developed in later life into an involvement in zoology, entomology, geology and also prehistory. In terms of the natural sciences, her researches led her to publish a number of articles, paint accurate illustrations of butterflies, moths and plants, and to correspond regularly with several important natural scientists. So, while many of her female contemporaries in the colonies might have sketched flowers and landscapes, sent packets of lobelia or pelargonium seeds home to England and cultivated gardens, Mary's participation in the dissemination of plants, seeds and information across the Empire was of a different order. Over the years, having acquired the discovering and collecting habit in earnest, she sent about a thousand specimens to the Herbarium of Trinity College in Dublin, and many others to the Royal Botanic Gardens at Kew. These days she is remembered taxonomically in the names of a number of plants and butterflies. The most charming is that of the smallest-known butterfly, the dwarf blue *Brephidium barberae*.[15]

The journal of her trek from Kimberley to Cape Town is not exclusively a work of natural history, as many of her other publications were, but I am not sure that her tale is what has been called a woman's story either. Certainly she recounted what she had seen in an engagingly conversational and humorous style, much cluttered with commas. She was concerned with details like the making of supper or the loss of a coffee kettle. She remarked on the facial expressions of her fellow travellers and servants, responded quite personally and empathetically to wild animals, and reflected on the possibilities of domesticating mockingbirds, vultures or suricates. Perhaps these could be evidence of a feminine eye. Otherwise, she shares some of her male predecessors' ways of seeing, sometimes even outdoing them in terms of colonial attitudes.

Like many of those who came before her on this route, Mary Barber was keenly interested in the unfamiliar environment through which she was travelling and expressed this through the collecting and naming of plants and creatures. In her case, her considerable knowledge of such things meant that she appreciated the theory of evolution. This in turn led her to question religious dogma quite adventurously. At the same time, her writing is a reminder of how even the gentle science of botanising imports into the colonies a grid of categories by which to see and name and rule. As a daughter of 1820 Settlers, she was generally approving of the settler impulse, and her description of the boer homestead quite naturally turns the Australian blue gum into a positive metaphor for the ineradicable tenacity of foreign stock:

> Strange to say, that almost without exception, one or two of the last named trees are planted on most South African farms; no matter how desolate or out of the way they may be, there will also be found this dark, solitary, exiled Australian; vanished from its native land, yet clinging to dear life with a tenacity surpassing that of the indigenous trees of the country.[16]

She then goes on to describe the trees as resilient pioneers in a tough environment, "pointing out, perchance, the desolation of the scene;

and yet bravely holding their own in spite of the vicissitudes of wind and weather". To this she adds, "I love bravery, even in the vegetable kingdom."[17]

Like other writers who passed through the region, she also experimented with a sort of amateur ethnography. After describing the farm in this way, she went on to report "the same old thing ad infinitum". For, as she put it, the Dutch homesteads, cast in the same mould, were all alike. The farmers too were all the same. Repeating the gist of many earlier explorers' stories of the boorishness of the Boers, she observed that there was never much speculation in their faces, that in these remote parts the inhabitants appeared to be steeped in hopeless ignorance and that indeed it was printed in large letters across their stolid countenances.[18]

As for the San, while certain of the earlier travellers (William Burchell, for instance) seem to have genuinely enjoyed the company of the indigenous people they met, and appreciated their language, Barber used an evolutionary model to voice a different point of view. Based on the imagined proximity of indigenous races to their poor relations who dwelt in trees, she confidently described Khoe-San languages as being like the chattering of baboons and monkeys.[19]

A hundred years later, it is easy for us to reject the naïveté and simple racism of this sort of attitude. Yet, in spite of the ways in which she reproduced some of the worst of contemporary prejudice, Mary Barber seems to me a thoughtful and sometimes original guide to the territory. In this case, her dubious theory certainly shows a colonial inability to recognise the humanity of other people. Still, she used it to make the more unusual suggestion that the threshold between humans and other animals is permeable and open to interpretation: "Some may not agree with me, perhaps, in calling the chatterings of *all* these creatures languages, but, as the different species individually understand each other sufficiently well, it is very difficult where to draw a line, or fix a landmark."[20] Another way of putting this would be to say, as some late modern people might now put it, that the natural world is full of culture.

Later, writing angrily against the widespread abuse of oxen which were forced to pull overloaded wagons across the country, she addressed the cattle directly:

> Alas, poor cattle! in your early youth the greater part of your natural food is appropriated to our use: no sooner have you arrived at the age of *oxenhood*, than to work upon the roads is your hard fate, where you may, perchance, be either beaten, or starved to death; whilst if you escape this doom, and live to be old, you are eventually fattened for the butcher, and remorselessly eaten by those for whom you have toiled and suffered. If there is a heaven for horned cattle – and I see no reason why there should not be . . . I believe their chances are infinitely greater than ours . . . I do not see why we should be so selfish as to claim for ourselves only, a future state: and what are we after all?[21]

What for us now is obviously absent from this tirade is any sign of compassion for the similar treatment of human servants, of which her particular travelling party had two, or of colonised people more generally. It would take JJR Jolobe's poem "The Making of a Servant", fifty years later, to face this pain directly in the memorable refrain: "*I have seen the making of a servant / in the young yoke-ox*".[22] Mary Barber did not consider servants in these terms. Yet the way she responded to animals may still be instructive for us now because she seems to have seen non-human animals as having personality and she tried to imagine their point of view.

This is not to say that the other travellers who passed through the territory never experienced awe or delight in meeting wild animals. Several writers described the astonishing abundance of springbok, the great migrations, thousands and thousands of them flocking across the land. As late as 1872, the distinguished geologist Edward John Dunn recorded in these words the wonder of a springbok migration he had seen in the Northern Cape:

> One may read about the vast numbers of springboks that migrate across this continent; but without seeing them no one can form a remote conception of their countless numbers. We have driven through them for six hours (35 miles); while from reliable information they extend for one hundred miles in length. Imagine from 2 000 to 6 000 of these animals scattered over the plain at intervals of two or three miles apart over the whole of

this area, and you may form some notion of their abundance. This is the most graceful of all the gazelles. They are the perfection of form, litheness and graceful action.[23]

He went on to write lyrically about the dazzling whiteness of the stripe along their bodies, about their exuberant playfulness and magnificent bounding leaps, about how pretty and saucy the beautiful little fawns are, about the wonder of seeing the whole herd galloping along at full speed, and he marvelled at how they bound and frisk and play, gambolling over the interminable plains, cropping a mouthful as required, living a life of freedom, having no care for the morrow. /Han≠kass'o is recorded as saying that the springbok resemble the water of the sea, and Dunn too described the grunts and movements of so many tens of thousands as being like the distant breaking of the sea on the rocks.

Yet, in all this, the countless antelope are also of course an easy source of meat. "How closely they allow us to approach!" Dunn wrote. "Sometimes within forty yards. Frequently they may be shot with a pistol from the cart."

Europeans may not have had the world monopoly on hunting animals to extinction. Yet one way or another by the end of the nineteenth century almost all the wild springbok, the gemsbok, the kudu and the other game, as they were called, had disappeared from the Northern Cape. Before this time, when the great springbok migrations galloped and gambolled through the land, it was good rains and tall new grass that called them. But once people carried guns, the buck were too easy a target, and when farmers moved in with multitudes of merino sheep, the long, golden grass was cropped short.

Now, besides the domesticated livestock which occupy the niche of many larger wild creatures in the system, those who remain are mostly little ones. A bat-eared fox lies crushed on the side of the road, a mongoose runs into the grass, a dassie watches the cars from a rock, still here. Witnessing their tracks and traces as we drive through, I feel some sparse hope of continuity, some glimpse of wildness, even on the farms.

As we drive on, the edges of the road are littered all the way with discarded cans and pieces of broken glass that twinkle like stars in the sun. Telephone poles accompany us and the clusters of concrete tables and chairs for roadside picnics have been freshly painted in yellow and green. Far from any city, the blue sky is traced with white jet trails. The wide land too is marked by cellphone aerials which the children call "pawks", a pointed spike that pokes or pawks upwards. Even so, the air does seem clear here and I imagine that the place recalls in fact some slow-paced spaciousness of mind before and beyond all this. To do just one thing in a day, even driving in a car on this straight road from dawn to dusk, is something wonderful. Krom, Brak, Sout, Orange, Modder, each river is a treasure in the desert. And all the way, the long quiet land. The veld still is, as they all say, vast.

Closer at last, much closer to Kimberley than to home, the road signs indicate battlefields. Belmont. Graspan. Modder River. Koffiefontein. Michael's grandfather, Carol Cope, and my mother's father, Alan Smallie, fought in the same regiment, the Natal Carbineers, in what they called the Boer War. Now stored carefully in a suitcase at the top of my mother's cupboard, my grandfather's letters to his parents tell his story of the Siege of Ladysmith: a tale of officers, bravery, dysentery and his beloved horse, Shandy. Later, and writing in a different voice, my paternal grandfather, AC Martin, also told stories of battles. He was a military historian, headmaster and colonel of the Durban Light Infantry, and I remember him working at his typewriter on the verandah of their flat in Durban in the 1960s, the desk laden with papers, manuscripts and dust. Yet surely we have not come this way to visit battlefields – even if these wars and the imperial male ancestors that they evoke may require some part in this journey that I do not yet understand.

On the long road the car fills up with stuff. Chip packets, sweet papers and biscuit crumbs, unravelling tapes which have become separated from their boxes, warmer clothes pulled off and flung into heaps at our feet, soft animals dressed and undressed, small coins counted and dropped under a seat. So far the children have managed not to bicker or whine, though they are hot and tired and cramped, and their humour may not last the journey. When they remember, they count garages. Engen, Caltex, all the big plastic signs. Fuel, toilets, food, the garage shop. Such things are a comfort on a journey.

Towards evening Sophie suddenly shouts, "Look, a bear!"

She is pointing to a telephone pole on which a huge nest has been built in the form of a giant teddy. A little further on, another nest takes the shape of a great grass bird, and on another pole the vague large mass is something the twins agree could be called a bearhive. We stop the car to get out and look at this wonder and watch the little birds flying in and out of the big communal home, and calling to one another in the late afternoon.

Philetarius socius, they are called, sociable weavers. The huge nests are the first of many that we see on this trip, and we come to love them: enormous grass houses hanging in trees and colonising telephone poles and pylons with a mass of grass stems, stacked and woven and patched together. Apparently each pair of birds and their chicks nestle in a separate compartment which is woven into the community of all the others. One nest may house as many as five hundred birds together, some of them different species that have come to join the colony. Now, at the end of the long, hot day when the sound of the car is stilled, we listen as the voices of many birds call to one another in the cooling evening. This, we imagine, is what they have always done. This is bird culture, bird society, hundreds of birds in the great nest, calling.

And now, continuing on and on towards our destination, the harsh sun gentled by dusk, the land is made of grasses and thorn trees, soft pale grass and darkening trees which evoke a longing for something that I cannot name. The early European explorers may have found the landscape of the interior impossibly brown and dry, but our first home is this savannah, and perhaps even now, in city parks and gardens, we may, in the mix of tree and mown green grass, recall some echo of its pattern. Now, travelling through in the changing dusk, I imagine the unkempt blond uncultivated grasses speaking of rain and the yearning for rain, of moisture gathering in the skies and the waves of springbok flowing through the land, of rain in the night and in the afternoons. Beyond the road signs, the back-lit thorn trees in the veld recall the FNB icon on my Petro Card. It looks like Africa.

I have booked a week's stay in a self-catering cottage on a farm near Kimberley, which we will use as a base for visiting the sites on our map. After journeying all day we arrive just before sunset to drive past rusting ossewa wheels at the gate and an impenetrable hedge of sisal.

"I've got little goats and ducklings for the children," the woman had said to me on the phone when I called her a while ago from Cape Town. "They'll love it."

It really did sound good, a nice retreat from the city, a farm. For a moment I forgot all about history and homesteads. Instead, the conversation brought to mind that fecund, wholesome farmyard I dreamed of as a child, a place of cows and sheep, milk in the morning and the fragrance of generation, fresh air and paddocks, straw and dung.

The actual farm is dry and scratchy, and the gumtrees look every bit as tenacious as in Mary Barber's unsympathetic description. The cottage where we are staying is an unquaint asbestos prefab, built close to the main house, with a family of goats living in the adjoining yard and a Labrador penned up in the muddy enclosure outside the kitchen. The dog picks up a bit of plastic pipe when we approach, then backs off, growling. A smaller dog follows Sophie inside and pisses on the carpet. Inside the farmhouse a large sjambok is hanging against the wall, yet the farmer is friendly and says the dogs are too.

"Just stay away from the pit bulls near the house," he cautions the children.

Someone has placed chocolates beside our beds, rusks and biscuits in the kitchen, and new soap and a vase of fresh cosmos in the bathroom. The prefab is decorated with care and my initial sense of discomfort seems churlish and judgmental. The bathroom smells of air freshener and there are frills on the toilet as well as on the toilet rolls and around the beds. In the lounge are a pair of eager china dogs, a leatherette sofa, ageing wall-to-wall carpets, a large television set and two big pink ornaments made of an extruded plastic that resembles the writhing flesh of many eels.

The woman was right too. Sophie and Sky do love it. In fact, they are intensely delighted by everything – dogs, goats, kittens, chickens, ducks, animals to talk to. Yet the drain of the kitchen sink is blocked, so that it is impossible to wash dishes, and when you run out the bath water, it flows straight through a broken pipe to join the chickens, the mud and the dog shit in the anxious Labrador's back yard. Parents do not like this sort of thing.

"I don't want to spend my holiday here," Michael says firmly.

His back is sore and he has been driving all day, worried that my more cautious pace would slow us down. At first I resist the idea of leaving, reluctant to face the farmer. Yet we have come a long way from city to country, from fynbos to thorn bushveld, in the hope that our journey might discover some quality of spaciousness, some memory of the land before guns and sheep and wire fences, of the environment here before all this. Now that we have arrived, I realise that to come with such expectations was naïve and thoughtless. The place is witnessing us, even as we interpret it. This recognition is chastening and ironic, even instructive. Still, suddenly it all feels just too difficult. I agree that we will have to move on.

In the morning I say to the farmer, "We really appreciate your kindness. You've been so warm. But you see, we're city people. When we come this far, we want to feel what open space is like. We don't want to be living with so many fences."

It is a half-truth, I suppose, yet good enough for us all to save face. The farmer seems unsurprised. Probably this has happened before. We pay the bill, shake hands and smile, and the white steam of our breath dissolves in the early winter air.

DIAMONDS

The faded black-and-white photograph at Reception depicts a sorrowful man who is naked except for a pair of thick mittens. One hand holds out eight large diamonds to the camera, while the other is covering his private parts. The text below explains that people were imprisoned here when they were suspected of swallowing diamonds, and that they had to remain naked until they had excreted them all. The prisoners had to wear the mittens to prevent them poking through the shit to find the treasure.

After leaving the farm we have checked in at a budget self-catering establishment in Kimberley called Gum Tree Lodge. The place was built as a convict station. In this it is like Breakwater Lodge, now a hotel and conference venue at the Cape Town Waterfront, that was previously the very Breakwater Prison where //Kabbo and the other /Xam prisoners were held. Although we do not mention this unpleasant history to Sophie and Sky, they complain that the place is not nearly as nice as where we have come from.

"We loved that farm," they insist, "with all the dogs and the little goats. We don't like it here. We want to go back."

To me, as well, the morning seems bleak and dreary, the bedrooms full of ghosts, prisoners again. But the rooms of our flatlet are clean and the management more professional. The plumbing works fine. The red stoep paint of the verandah is polished, and the spiral broekielace at the edge of the corrugated iron roofs looks pretty. Someone is taking care of the garden and there are swings and a jungle gym. Perhaps the photograph of the prisoner indicates some attempt to face what happened in the past. It will be all right.

Because the appointments I have made begin the following day, we unpack the car and set off to discover Kimberley, the city that sparkles.

From the brochures we have collected it seems that tourist information for the region must always include at least one picture of the Big Hole. This is diamond country after all, diamantveld, its story told in images of discovery and digging, photographs of the Hole and of brilliant-cut diamonds. The tale of how an unmarked kopje in the veld became in July 1871 the precious destination for a great rush of fortune seekers from around the world. Digging, excavating, grinding, dumping – in a few brief years their hopeful shovels and great machineries constructed this city with the tools of this desire. As one might expect, though many of those who did the work were black men from the villages, most stories of the early days tell of white miners who came from Cape Town, America, England, Australia and so on. The visitor meets this history everywhere in photographs, cartoons and cheery icons of the digger and the small man's quest, stories of grit and dust, of sheer determination. But it was not long before those bearded and grubby individuals were edged out of their claims, and a single company of mining magnates and millionaires became owner and guardian of the treasure. In a short while the kopje itself was displaced by a stony absence, said to be the biggest hole ever dug with pick and shovel.

And certainly it is big. We stand with a group of other tourists on the little fenced-off platform to look over the edge. Down, down, grey rock, down. Water at the bottom reflects the sky. There is grey dust at our feet, and on the grass, and powdering the thorn trees around the edge. As a middle-aged tannie explains with gloomy relish, the fence is there because of suicides. Imagine falling into that deep pit of sky. Imagine all those men, digging. Imagine the grey dust in their clothes and their lungs. Imagine the multitude of ropes and pulleys. Over the forty or so years that it was mined, the Big Hole yielded, as they say, 2 722 kilograms of diamonds.[24]

"Did only men do it, digging for diamonds?" Sophie asks.

"I suppose so, wouldn't you think?"

Certainly there was at least one woman in the early years who took a practical interest in the diggings, though not primarily because of diamonds. Aside from her views on the personhood of animals, what really distinguishes Mary Barber's stories of wanderings in the interior is her fascination with stone artefacts. She was one of the first people to recognise and document the significance of the mass of worked stone tools in the Northern Cape. Her journal describes spearheads, arrow-heads, scrapers and knives in some detail, while correctly identifying the tiny San tools as being more recent than the ancient handaxes. In the diamond claims at Kimberley she recognises the stone artefacts that others tossed aside in search of diamonds, and she tells how seeing and holding these stone tools in her hands evokes a sense of deep time and prehistoric human culture which qualifies her view of recent history and its priorities. Thinking presumably of the dating of Creation and the Garden of Eden at 4004 BC, she writes, "What are 6 000 years in the chronology of the world's history when compared with the lithography scattered over its face?"[25]

But there is nothing in the official information at the mine that calls to mind this woman's story of the place, or recalls the abundance of artefacts she saw. Instead, a sign informs us that during the Siege of Kimberley, which began four days after the start of the Anglo-South African Boer War, hundreds of women and children were lowered into the mine for safekeeping. The information evokes a picture of lace and starched white bonnets, the anxious bodies of women and girls and boys, of dirt and dust. Now that their voices are long dead, the Hole is simply big and grey and silent, a sort of emptiness. In a quick flash of gold against the grey, a mongoose pauses to look at us, quick small body light as fur.

At the mining museum Sky finds a great black machine that moves and grinds when you put money in the slot. Sophie and I use up our coins on a wonderful miniature diorama which changes, through the magic of mirrors and reflected light, from a model of the original kopje into a model of the Big Hole, then back again to the kopje: before and after, before and after, before and after. On a map of claims and in one of the group photographs Michael searches for his ancestor EBJ Knox, who owned a piece of the Big Hole in the early years. But he cannot find him. These gentlemen with moustaches all look the same, and the leather-bound share registers and ledgers are heavy with names.

After milkshakes at the faux Victorian restaurant, we take a trip to the city and back in the real antique tram with its polished art nouveau brass fittings and finely turned oak seats. The ride goes from the Big Hole around the perimeter of the mine, the edge planted with dusty sisal and other spiky and inhospitable aliens, past the building of the Flash Funeral Society and the words "TOMBSTONES GRAFSTENE" in big orange-and-yellow plastic letters, past modern buildings from the 1960s, now fallen into disrepair. The children are excited, chatting to the driver and dashing among the seats. After a short stop we return to the mine.

Back at the outdoor museum we look through the windows of the De Beers Railway Coach that was used by directors of the company for traversing the country. Peering in, you can see sparkling crystal glasses and cut-glass bottles of sherry, a table laid with silver spoons, and a real bath. As we gaze in through the glass, this ordered world looks tooled and polished, the sealed compartments in which they ate and talked and washed and slept, rich coach travelling through the desert.

Although we may not recognise them in the photographs, traces of those ancestors who were here before remain in the massive mining headgear, the heavy machineries and dark locomotives, things made of iron and steel and sent across the world to excavate the treasure. The empty mine is quiet now, but in a reconstructed village the Digger's Rest is full of drinking songs, a church plays hymns, and an empty wrought-iron bandstand still sounds the disembodied music of a jolly band on a summer's afternoon.

The children dart about the dusty place like swallows, up the steps and down again, through the doors and out, then into a portable pressed-iron ballroom that was once shipped out to the colony. The white ceiling is divided into squares and studded with golden stars and fleurs-de-lis, with a cluster of gold flowers at the centre, surrounded by electric lights shining out of other flowers and a frieze of more fleurs-de-lis around the edge.

The afternoon light shines through high windows onto pressed-iron walls which once were sky-blue. But the ballroom is empty of dancers in evening gowns and pretty shoes, the lovely fire of gemstones against their skin. It is empty of dancing gentlemen in well-cut suits, empty of girls and watching mothers, and young men tanned from the African sun. From an invisible tape the Fourth Movement of Schubert's *Trout Quintet* recalls the spiralling dance of men and women here, the sweat and longing of their arms, feet swept in time to music, the ballroom lit with electricity, gold flowers spiralling among the stars. Now, in the afternoon dust, their dresses hang on cold mannequins in tall glass cases. The painted blue-sky walls record the dirt and pressures of a hundred years, their patterns rubbed.

Like a pang of love, the Schubert recalls to me my father, how he delighted in that piece of music and taught me to listen to it. Listen to the trout, he would say, pointing out the song of its joy which repeats without repeating the song of water and light and swimming fish. He too is long gone now, but hearing again the exuberance of this music in a dusty room, I imagine that in some river yet the trout dances upstream.

Though the music pulls at my heart, my own children soon tire of the ballroom. Laughing, they caper out together into the grey streets of the mining museum to skip past shops full of things, artefacts cluttered together to reconstruct a past, or fix in place the constant flow of change and summon up a sense of loss. I point out the lacy bonnets, bibs and baby shoes of other children, and a collection of grey suits, silk stockings, drapery and imported shawls. Look at the old medicines, and the spectacles and the ceramic hot water bottle. See what care they took in the making of hat pins, christening dresses, striking clocks and ostrich-feather fans, these things they gathered to make a life, precious things, bought with money from the mine, a clutter of things in the veld.

Searching among this curious assemblage for some live trace of the people who once used these things, I pause at a shop window stacked with ladies' footwear. The shoes are all dainty and high-heeled, made of fine, tooled leather, white or red or tan or even striped, adorned with a little bow or a buckle, and with a space for the toes to peep out. The shoes are arranged in tiered concentric circles on little glass stands, and high in the centre of the display rests a pair of golden slippers, flanked by silver sandals on either side. For a moment I can almost sense the legs and feet that wore them and left in each the shape of their particular tread: beautiful feet, held tight in the clasp of dainty leather, feet walking and dancing, feet that sweated and ached and are no more, having left behind a throng of shoes. The window glass reflects my own two feet in flat old sandals, dusty feet too big to fit those Cinderella shoes.

Across the way at the Shilling Aerated Water Factory a waxwork black man operates a machine for putting aerated water into bottles. He is opaque and lifeless as a waxwork, but the empty oval-shaped bottles have a quality of translucence. Laid out in rows in the window, each one is decorated with a glass dog or shamrock, an antlered buck or a motif of three running legs connected at the thigh, unshattered greeny glass misted with time, with a marble stopper at the neck. Each person who drank water from these bottles was thirsty in the heat and dust, and their breath, like ours, made steam on a winter's morning. The shape of the empty bottles left behind is sensuous, simple: the form of useful things once made with care by hand, each one distinct and like the others, a pattern which repeats without repeating.

Did the waxwork man ever drink this water? And the prisoner who had swallowed diamonds? A single dark and indistinct photograph depicts "Kimberley Before the Discovery of Diamonds". Iconic, instructive, the picture shows the kopje, an acacia tree, the open thornveld, and a half-naked black man in silhouette, holding upright a stick or a spear. A caption points out the sociable weavers' nests in the tree.

Back in the modern city, lemon and olive trees now laden with fruit have been planted along the roadsides for anyone to pick. Beyond their reach the billboards advertise in discreet and elegant lettering a myth of permanence and power, of something more lasting than this impermanent fruitfulness: "De Beers / A diamond is forever".

I remember that for the First People of the Kalahari and others campaigning against the dispossession and forced removal of the G//ana and G/wi people from diamond-rich areas of the Central Kalahari Game Reserve in Botswana, this very slogan became a source of irony and a focus of their critique. Perhaps a diamond can last for ever, they said, but it seems that people are disposable.

And now, after a day in Kimberley, we have seen a mass of things and consequences but not one diamond. The heart of the place is lost or hidden in a shell of stories and accumulated stuff. Each one of us is tired, our skin coated grey. My body aches and my heart yearns for sweetness, for the sweet good land before and beyond.

Perhaps Mary Barber had similar emotions. At the beginning of her *Wanderings* she described the relief she felt on leaving behind the industrial noise and waste of the mining town, which was then only eight years old:

> The loud dynamite blasting in the various mines, the continuous din of machinery, the voices of many tongues and languages, which, like the sound of the sea, were ever in our ears, – all these accustomed sounds had become conspicuous by their absence . . . it was a joy that we could scarcely realise, a new feeling, and we breathed freely, for were we not out on the wide plains, beyond the range of sardine tins, broken bottles, and the innumerable cases which once contained preserved meats, and in fact, beyond the range of the debris of the great town.[26]

Like her, I want to reach beyond this industry and dust. Perhaps we can even find some water. In one of the brochures I notice a picture of a pan called Kamfersdam. Flamingos live there, it says, about a quarter of the South African population of these birds. We decide to go and have a look.

The road is the N12 to Johannesburg, fast and fairly busy. There is a garage on one side and the Flamingo Casino nearby. Suddenly a pink flowering of flamingos blooms on the water of the pan, thousands and thousands of pink bird flowers drifting together on the water, bright sweet lotuses blooming in the dusty land. As we stand on the edge of the road, cars roar by, and the voices of a myriad pink flamingos chatter in the water beyond, a field of long, thin necks and legs, birds flying in thousands and standing in the water, chattering. Pink as roses or the cheeks of children flushed with sleep or play, this right here is the lotus land of pink flamingos, lively flowering of birds and water. Joy.

As we drive back to the city, I feel reluctant to return. But Michael, who is a jeweller, says, "It's not just about money and greed, you know. If you want to understand, you need to really *look* at some diamonds."

The only diamonds we have seen so far are fakes and pictures. Eureka, Cullinan, Jonker: replicas of the famous jewels twinkle behind glass. Ideas, not things. The real diamonds that I know are smaller treasures, set in gold or silver, worn on wrists and fingers, or at the heart. When I was a child the diamond in my mother's engagement ring was our only precious stone. When it fell out in town one day, leaving an empty hole like a pulled tooth, I remember how lost she felt, not wanting my father to see. Later I inherited a swirling art nouveau ring from my aunt Madge which I used to wear until it too disappeared.

Now these particular stones are lost to us, but there is still a pendant my mother wears for special occasions. After her eldest sister died, she asked Michael to make something new for her from all the old rings. So he melted down the silver and gold from Letty's engagement ring and her own wedding band, and made from them a golden tree, set with diamond flowers, a garden of twinkling, rose-cut stars and little birds to hang on a silver chain around her neck.

In a sense then, each diamond we have worn bears dreams and stories. Or perhaps each precious stone invokes into being the particular forms of prisons, churches and museums, of glass bottles, music, money, dancing shoes and sardine tins, of labourers, prisoners and ladies, grey dust and noise, of dispossession, forced removals and resistance, of wanting and not wanting, wealth and pain, desire and power and loss, and all of this city in the veld. In this respect a diamond is quintessentially a thing of culture, excavated from the earth and faceted, full of human tools and history and all the machineries of our time. Looking at a diamond in this way is like looking into a mirror: a clear, hard stone, which will endure somewhere in the world long after Kimberley is gone, retaining in its form and cut some trace of the flickering transience of these years, this place.

This is one way of looking at diamonds. From another view the adamantine clarity of a diamond evokes an image of that which goes beyond our history and desire. Although it is cut and formed by human tools, the artefact made from this hard stone seems undefiled by that which it reflects: a crystal mirror in which all things arise and pass away again. The jewel is clear as water, empty as the sky, radiant in the evanescent light and colours of the world.

And then there is the shimmering. In the dancing ballroom light the diamonds shimmer and sparkle like the stars, and the jewelled star-light shines like magic at midday. In our darkness we long for light and stars to adorn our bodies, diamonds on our fingers or at the heart. Twin-kling or burning brighter than any other stone, this thing we love is shimmering starlight against our flesh, an inextinguishable fire. Ah.

Having returned from Kamfersdam and diamonds to Gum Tree Lodge, I find that I still want something more.

"Let's go and see the sunset, feel the place wild."

We all pick our way to the edge of the fence to watch the pink fla-mingo light turn to darkness across the veld. Suddenly from beyond the thorn trees comes the sound of gunshots.

"What's that noise?" Sky asks immediately.

"Gunshots. It's shooting."

"What are they shooting? Can we go and see? Why are they shoot-ing?" He is excited, scared.

"Probably just practising," I say. "They like it. No, we can't go and see. They might shoot us by mistake. They wouldn't mean to, of course. It's Sunday, so probably they don't have to work. They're just having fun."

Once back at our rooms, the twins find a treasure more perfect to them than any precious stone. It is a puppy, a tiny dachshund dressed in a winter jacket, which belongs to the managers. Sophie and Sky kiss him and cuddle him and together they carry him awkwardly across the lawn, prancing and shouting with happiness, or stopping to crouch with the puppy on the grass, to hug and snuggle.

"Mommy, you just have to come and stroke him," they say. "He's the sweetest, the cutest, the most darlingest puppy you can think of. And we've changed our minds now about Gum Tree Lodge. It's the best place ever."

MUSEUM

At ten o'clock in the morning there is nobody to meet us at the McGregor Museum. There is nobody around in the great entrance hall, two storeys high, or on the wide red-carpeted staircase of the grand old building, designed in high Victorian style as a sanatorium for ladies and gentlemen of the Empire.

During the Siege of Kimberley, Rhodes had his quarters here, and they are said to have been spartan for someone of his stature. The building was busy then, a node of urgencies, pleasures and communications. But now we wander through empty, unattended rooms, the pressed white ceilings decorated with golden stars, the stained-glass windows lit with morning pinks and greens, and a Steinway on a polished floor waiting for the touch of fingers on the ivories again. At last, somewhere upstairs in a back office behind a door which says "No Entry", I find a woman working at a desk.

"You're looking for David Morris?" she says. "Is he expecting you? I'll call him at the site."

David is the head of archaeology at the museum. In his last email he said, "I write with one foot in the grave," and told about excavating a mass burial site which had recently been uncovered in Kimberley. Municipal workers had been digging a storm-water trench when they found some human remains. At first, he said, they had carried on digging regardless, ripping skeletons out of rest from 180 metres of unmarked graves, and dumping tons of the trench material somewhere out of sight, where the bones were then unobtrusively crushed into the ground. Then someone had tipped off the museum about what was happening, and at once the place became an archaeological site – or rather a salvage site using archaeological techniques – and the City, in compliance with heritage law, undertook to fund its investigation.

Now, waiting for David, we roam about among the exhibits. A few dead old stuffed animals stare into the beyond with glass-bead eyes, and a sociable weavers' nest, a big one, hangs suspended with little dead birds dangling about on strings, as though leaving and entering, as though to represent the whirr of culture, the complex etiquettes of mating and dwelling, of foraging and inhabiting.

The children's excited response reminds me of the delight of visiting the Natal Museum in Pietermaritzburg when I was a child. Although the great halls did smell dead and dusty, the wonderful scary hippopotamus stood at the entrance with its pink painted mouth wide open, there were rooms full of wild creatures and upstairs you could see the chicken with three legs and other curiosities behind glass. Afterwards there was often a currant bun, and perhaps my cousins had come with us for the afternoon.

Now the animals in natural history museums seem to me rigid with horror, poor stuffed beings, the leap of their joy frozen into a single gesture. The fur, the skin, the shell or the feet may be more or less intact, patched and stitched together. But that is all that remains. For the rest, inside and outside the skin, nothing is left behind of the sentient body, alive in a real environment among other bodies. The smell is gone, and the eyes are cold. Inside the skin it is empty, filled with the stuffing of the taxidermist's art. Outside, extracted from the world of plants and earth and rocks and water and other beings that gave it life, the skin of each one stands or lies or crouches among the unfamiliar assembled dead, the big animals often collected together, elephants and camels, then primates in one case, fierce cats in another, and smaller animals from many different regions packed into a single imaginary environment, a single eternity, bodies turned to the glass, arranged to fit. As we walk together now past the creepy assembly of once living beings, I wonder about the circumstances in which they were killed and reconstructed for display. The animals are dead, very dead, but each one has been posed and formed to repeat a familiar story, each one is turned to face the viewer as we pass, glass eyes fixed in an eternal stare.

In the 1870s, several of Wilhelm Bleek's /Xam informants were brought to the Iziko South African Museum in Cape Town to identify and sometimes tell stories about animals, birds and insects as part of the recording process. These visits were unrelated to the subsequent construction of the contentious Bushman diorama (now closed to the public), for which people identified as being "pure Bushmen" on the basis of appearance and language were used to make the body casts illustrating their type. But in retrospect those meetings in the 1870s of people and animals, dead and living beings, seem poignant and somehow emblematic.

On different visits the informants named Hyena Billosa, Wilde Hond, Leopard, Male Lion and Female Lion, Hippopotamus, Giraffe, Elephant, Male Springbok, Spotted Hyena, Artel, Rheebuck, Wild Cat, Lynx, Porcupine, Rabbit, Hare, Cape Anteater, Zebra, Duiker, Klip Springer, Springbok, Gemsbok, Steenbok and Dog. They said the words for Mouse, Squirrel, Ostrich, Common Quail, Greywing Partridge, Blue Crane, Striped Hyena, Flamingo. They said Mantis, "Walking Stick" Insect, Common Cape Dragon Fly, Great Cape Sand Wasp, Butterflies, Death's Head Moth, Tsetse Fly, Cape Winged Horse Tick. //Kabbo said, "The Jackal here sits looking", and /Han≠kass'o told a story about clapping hands and speaking to the Withered Leaf Insect, a creature that taxonomy enigmatically calls *Phyllomorpha paradoxa*. [27]

A hundred and thirty years later, the natural history exhibit at Iziko is a favourite with Sophie and Sky. They love the male gorilla who bares his teeth in fury, and the vixen and her cubs cuddled together on the ground, baby foxes playing and rolling in the sand. Gerbils stand cutely on two back legs and a baby zebra nuzzles its mother. A roaring hippo's huge pink mouth is open wide, and beside it is a big, sad, wrinkled elephant cow. Most of them look old, but the Cape hare and the endangered riverine rabbit are particularly tatty. I have read in the Bleek-Lloyd Archive that one must not say the name of a lion, and that children in particular should be careful of being disrespectful, for the lion will not forget this behaviour when the child is grown, and he will come to find him. But the lion preserved behind the glass smells only of dust and chemicals, and the scent and person of lion are gone. Behind this glass the lion is finally bound and still. Above the heads of other animals, long separated from the great waves of his companions on the grassland, a single springbok springs, suspended forever with nylon thread.

Whenever I visit with the twins there is an uncanny resonance in the recognition that some of the exhibits we are looking at are the very stuffed animals which //Kabbo, /A!kunta and /Han≠kass'o saw and named. Did they sense some correspondence between the taxidermic impulse of natural history and Bleek's preservation of their words and stories before they became extinct? It is not recorded and cannot be re-membered what they might have felt about the lion or springbok they named, or about the other assemblages of skin, teeth, paws and tawny furs preserved in these halls.

Now in natural history museums the parties of excited schoolchil-dren pass and point at the animals, laughing. I wonder whether it is possible for the dead old artefacts, displaced things, to recall for them even in a small voice the warm flanks and quivering noses of creatures that once were wild. Seeing these tired things, traces removed from their relations, can any of them conceive of what is lost? Can they re-cognise for a moment in the stitched-up skins the wildness of animal beings or their continuities with our kind? These days I want to cry and shout, to break the glass, pull the poor old animal ghosts outside and bury them.

At the McGregor Museum the small collection of stuffed animals leads on to the Ancestors' Gallery, a reputedly well-told representation of the last three million years in the Northern Cape. Near the entrance is a reconstruction of *Australopithecus africanus*, an early hominid ancestor, whose dates centre around 2.8 million years ago. The name is the one that Raymond Dart gave to a fossil discovered in 1924 at Taung, not far from Kimberley. It was the skull of a child about Sophie and Sky's age, with a full set of baby teeth and the six-year molars just beginning to erupt, as theirs are. The Taung child had a relatively small brain, but its teeth were human-like, and it walked upright.

In retrospect, this find changed irrevocably the way our ancestry was understood. But it took more than twenty years for the vituperative palaeoanthropological establishment in Britain to accept its significance. One reason for this was that the Taung child contradicted the evidence of what was called Piltdown Man, and challenged the ideology it was being used to promote. The Piltdown skull, dug up in 1912 and proved only forty years later to have been a hoax, was a combination of a human skull and the jaw of an ape. Described approvingly as the first Englishman, it had a pleasingly large brain which seemed to confirm the idea of Cartesian human beings' ascendancy over other animals. For if in the process of evolution our brains got big before the teeth lost the fierce power of their canine bite, one might be able to believe that the mind was leading the body upwards: I think, therefore

I am a human being. Instead, what the Taung skull shows is a being who is walking upright as we do and chewing food as we do. Because of this, it is what is called a hominid, a member of the human family, an ancestor. But the brain of the australopithecines is not yet very developed. Relative to their body size, their brains were small, and although they were bipedal, they were also good climbers and probably built nests in trees. In a sense they were people and in another sense they were animals.

The image of *Australopithecus africanus* in the glass case at the museum is short, shaggy and rather bestial, his expression simple-minded. Suggesting his transitional, in-between status in the story of evolution, he appears to us now emerging into the light at the threshold of a backdrop of dark forest, while the two-dimensional painted female of the species still stands behind him in the shadows, carrying a baby. The male holds a stick and has just bashed a grim and very reptilian leguaan with a piece of rock, leaving red paint blood all around.

"Poor lizard!" say Sophie and Sky crossly.

Progressing to the right, the next hominid on display is called *Homo rhodesiensis*, a kind of person more recently subsumed under the category *Homo heidelbergensis,* or an archaic form of *Homo sapiens,* and thought to be between 300 000 and 600 000 years old. Here he stands in the foreground of a spacious diorama of pale blue sky and light clouds, the murky forest left behind and the wide, wide world extending at his back. Hairless except for long dreads, he is built like a powerfully muscled superhero, with a fierce, strange face. He wears a loincloth and wields above his head a sharpened stick, which he is using to kill a stuffed bushpig.

"Poor pig! Oh, poor pig! Horrible man! Stop killing that pig!" shout the children, who love all mammals.

Is this our man, the person who made the handaxes at Kathu that we have come all this way to see? If the stuffed animals in the previous room seem far removed from the living beings whose skins they wear, then how much more these hominid figures built on the evidence of a few fossil bones must embody the imaginations of the people who constructed them.

When killing, conquering and devouring appear as the dominant metaphors for being a human, then the club-wielding caveman must always be dragging his woman away to the cave, and the stone arte-facts he left behind can only be weapons or tools for butchering. So when Raymond Dart interpreted the fossil assemblages he found in South Africa, the Taung child and others, he notoriously concluded that our australopithecine ancestors had been fierce, ruthless, carniv-orous killers who tore their living prey apart, devouring the hot blood and the dismembered writhing flesh. Writing in the immediate post-war period in response to what he called the slaughter-gutted archives of history, Dart discovered something that he believed must be in-herent in human beings, a nature that is predisposed to violence and aggression, a feature of hominid ancestry that separates us from our relatives among the apes. Later researchers came to show that the aus-tralopithecines were in fact more often the prey of other animals than the bloodthirsty carnivores he imagined, the hunted rather than the hunters. But Dart's point of view had a certain appeal, and authors such as Robert Ardrey came to popularise the idea of a human nature whose evolutionary beginnings made us essentially violent. In spite of later publications, this idea tends to recur.

Now at the *Australopithecus* display a group of schoolchildren crowd towards the glass while a teacher explains this hairy ancestor to them.

"Kinders," she says authoritatively, "dit is Die Aapman."

But what is an ape and what can it teach us about being a man, a human being? In the late 1960s, Jane Goodall's study of chimpanzees at Gombe led her to describe our closest nonhuman relations as the living link between man and beast. After she had recorded chimps using tools to get food or water, later research looked further into their use of tools, analysed aspects of their material culture, and even excavated assemblages of chimpanzee stone artefacts for comparison with early hominid sites. Work of this kind suggests wonderful analogies for understanding *Homo sapiens*, and for imagining our common ancestors. But, like Dart's postwar conclusions about *Australopithecus*, research into nonhuman primates has often tended to discover social orders that confirm what the researcher already suspected about human beings. Some scientists have observed male-dominance hierarchies without which everything falls apart, primate groups maintained by the power of aggressive male individuals and defined by their hunting. Others, often women, have asked different questions and told different stories about nonhuman primates, stories of the mother-centred units in which children are raised, of foraging, gathering, sharing and co-operation.[28]

Among our chimpanzee cousins, for example, the two different species of chimp have been interpreted to suggest different metaphors for human origins. On the one hand, the so-called common chimpanzee, *Pan troglodytes*, is described as having social groupings in which close-knit associations of females and their children tend to forage separately from males, while some rather aggressive all-male parties defend the communal territory. This has led some authors to see the encounters between males among common chimpanzees as evidence for the roots of human violence. On the other hand, it has been argued that the last common ancestors of human beings and apes may have been more like *Pan paniscus*, the pygmy chimpanzees or bonobos. Their habitat supplies more abundant food than that of the other species; they seem to form more cohesive, peaceful and sociable groups, where there is no need for males to band together for defence, and females are said to be influential throughout the social order, apparently choosing love (or rather sexual social relations) over war. This sort of founding myth certainly seems more appealing. But if the bodies of other animals recall to us a human story, and if our narratives are written into the bones and stones we discover, how may we ever know?

Here at the McGregor Museum the halls are populated with things arranged behind the glass to show and tell and teach. First the stuffed animals reside together in an eternal present, a place outside history. Then the story of evolution, our current creation myth, is like the beginning of linear time, its narrative of artefacts and apemen a spatial map of the progress of our species through the years. This leads at last to the minute specificity of recorded histories in the Northern Cape. In this long walk from handaxes to diamonds and the present moment, our human mind, awakening to the blue dawn of a diorama sky, seems to be made of a questioning wonder that is as unanswerable and as ineradicable as desire. Who was here before? What is our nature? Why am I suffering? How can I be happy?

Perhaps the museum could invite contemporary artists to bring some other myths and installations to the collection. I think of the life-size sculpture of three ominous lowering men with horns which became a well-known icon of the apartheid regime's coercive power during the 1980s. It was made by Jane Alexander and called *The Butcher Boys*. Since then, she has done several more representations of animal people, of people who are animals, haunting assemblages of sad and tender primates, of children, dogs. Walking now among the liminal spaces of the Ancestors' Gallery, I am reminded of this work, and of one sculpture in particular called *Bom Boys*. I believe it was made when the artist's own son was a little boy, and that the title refers to graffiti seen on a Cape Town wall – a gang sign, perhaps.

In the South African National Gallery in Cape Town, another branch of Iziko, where I happened upon the sculpture with Sophie and Sky, we found the small boys standing together and alone on the gallery floor in tones of grey and pale, nine little persons with rabbit face, hyena, dog. Animal ears. Their heads all reached to the height of my hip, more or less the height of Dart's little Taung child. But these were modern boys, boys who were animals with soft, expectant ears and pointed noses, little animals who were boys in laced-up shoes, boys who were naked or clothed, animals with light shoulder blades and delicate open hands.

Like figures in a diorama, Alexander's nine small animal boys are artefacts, things of fibreglass and wood, of culture, cloth, synthetic clay and paint. They are imaginary things, like fragments of a dream. Yet in the memory they seem to me livelier than any stuffed animal or hominid reconstruction I have seen in a museum. Each form is silent, poignant, strange. Each form speaks of the tenderness of wrists and knees, of scapula and collarbone. Their eyes are glass, yet they seem almost alive, gazing towards us and beyond, for ever.

In an obvious sense the Ancestors' Gallery at the McGregor Museum has been constructed to respond to questions of origins. But where the mine museum is stacked with a multitude of shoes and bottles, here a few choice things must tell three million years. This extraordinary story is situated in the old sanatorium as a sort of bridge between taxonomy and the colonial wars, between natural and cultural history, between sociable weavers and Cecil John Rhodes.

But nowhere in these polished halls is the transition from images and stories of animals to representations of people presented as an object of interest or inquiry in itself. What does it mean for nature to become culture? Or when does animal become person? And how can we tell? Perhaps such questions are not the business of a museum. For here the words and figures behind the glass are separate, distinct and motionless, and the shifting indeterminacy of things and beings remains unsaid.

I think again of the little *Bom Boys*, whose presence evokes a time when animals were people, and people were animal. The Taung child, *Australopithecus africanus, Homo erectus, Homo ergaster, Homo sapiens*, our kind. Countless generations on, the human hands still work the stone, the clay, the metal and other materials, make artefacts and art and put them in the fire. Bodies give birth. The light breath moves from mother to child. Metaphors and stories take form in the mind. The sentient animal boys are shaped like this from things our hands have made, a mother's hands, remembering.

Before we have time to look closely at the halls of more recent history, a bear-shaped man appears quietly from a back room somewhere. Clear blue eyes, a dark beard, a reticent smile. It must be David. We shake hands, introduce everyone.

"Let's go out to the site and talk there," he says.

Though this is not what I would have chosen, meeting at the site of the burial ground seems somehow appropriate. As Bertie and Victor Peers found, human remains have been some of the key treasures that archaeologists hope to unearth, and museums to collect. They are also, for obvious reasons, the most sensitive and vulnerable to abuse. At both the McGregor Museum and Iziko in the early years of the twentieth century, bones of known "Bushman" people were purchased under the most dehumanising circumstances, and until fairly recently some of these were actually still on display.[29] A hundred years later, the accidental discovery of colonial burials beneath this modern city revealed among other things a curious synchronicity. The Kimberley bones came to light only a fortnight before the first of what proved to be a great assembly of previously unknown human remains were exhumed in Cape Town after workers on a development site in Prestwich Place came upon human skeletons. Are these bones artefacts? Or are they ancestors? And under what conditions might they be both? These are questions that the archaeological theorist Nick Shepherd subsequently came to ask about the exhumation of the site. But that, perhaps, could be another story – though the grids and trowels, the brushes, buckets and sieves involved are similar instruments of investigation.[30]

We stop the car at the side of a dusty road at the edge of Kimberley between the Gladstone cemetery and a De Beers mine, where a long channel has been cut in the hard ground. The rescue site is marked out in squares with string and nails. Sitting in an opened, damaged grave is the former museum director, archaeo-zoologist Liz Voigt, gently removing the earth with a small trowel from around three skeletons.

"The teeth are very good," she remarks. "Good dentition, no cavities. Must have been poor people."

"What makes you say that?"

"They didn't have much sugar. Couldn't afford it."

"And how long do you think they've been here?"

"Probably about a hundred years," David says. "It seems they needed to bury them quickly – a mass burial. We're not sure why. Maybe the Spanish flu or the Siege of Kimberley."

"I see. And what else can you tell about them?"

"They're probably black people. We found some bits of jewellery, copper bracelets and earrings."

"Would they have buried black people separately from whites?"

"Clearly so, I think, around that time."

If they had died at home in the villages, they might have been laid to rest in a foetal position not far from the living, bodies buried under the soft dung floor of a cattle kraal, families sleeping among ancestors, ancestors inhabiting the place, returning. But here in the city that sparkles, the human beings were heaped like rubbish into unremembered graves, far from home. I wonder if the waxwork man from the Shilling Aerated Water Factory is here, or the prisoner who swallowed diamonds. The skeletons' teeth are perfect, their mouths open wide, as if calling out.

David explains that the rest of the team involved in the excavation are a group of unemployed people from the Kimberley community. In contrast with the conflicts of interest that the excavation of the Prestwich site in Cape Town generated, the circumstances here are different, and the situation has been handled differently. There has been no pressure from big business to clear the land for development, nobody from any community claiming knowledge of or personal interest in the graves, and apparently no significant polarisation between professionals, field workers and other people. David says that several of the helpers whom they have taken on are showing an interest in continuing work in archaeology in the future, and that Kimberley people generally see this as an opportunity to get to the bottom of a buried history. Today the rest of the team are down at the nearby dump, sieving for parts of skeletons that were tipped out with ground from the trench.

"It's a calamity," he says, "but some good may come of it."

Meanwhile, Liz sits peacefully in the grave, taking out sand and gravel with a trowel, or brushing away sediment from the bones and tipping it into a bucket for sieving. Standing together, adults and children, we watch as tibia and femur emerge from the earth, just the bones left now, no flesh or muscle, just the pale limbs lying in the shape of a human body. A hundred years or more they slept in this earth, bones resting quietly in the form of a human being. Soon, after measuring and counting, the throng of quiet bones will be put into bags, sorted and labelled for further study at the museum. Later they will be buried again, with the participation of the community. Perhaps someone will yet discover them as ancestors.

Remembering Bertie Peers and his father at Fish Hoek, their diggings and detonations and stories of ancient little men, I ask David what happens when a place becomes a site. He does not answer my question directly, but explains that the more care you take, the better information you can derive. He says that at the Gladstone cemetery they are interested in finding out about the lives and last moments of the people who were buried there, what rites of passage, if any, there might have been. I remember the little baby that Bertie describes finding wrapped in leaves and soft buckskin, and the young woman wearing her bags of precious stones and herbs, garlanded with thousands of beads and painted with ochre.

David's face tenses. "Though what rites could there have been here, in such circumstances? Or rights, for that matter, human rights. The corpses were almost literally dumped in crowded graves, up to ten in one."

He explains that down in the grave the body liquids flow and chemicals do things to bone. The archaeological study of what is called taphonomy involves interpreting the markers of this change, how things decompose and disintegrate, how deep underground the living processes begin, continue and are to some extent interrupted by the dig, how roots of shrubs and trees find their way down, growing into the folds of scapulas and along limbs.

Right now the morning is windy, dust blown into our faces from the excavated graves. Standing about and listening to David, watching that Sophie and Sky behave appropriately, and observing the delicate frontier of excavation, the quiet brushing away of earth from bone, dry bones in the earth, I find that the grave is strangely emptied of fear. This thing is what we human beings tend to dread: this is death and skeletons, impermanence, decay. Yet here not even the children are afraid. Perhaps it is the objectifying gaze of archaeology that empties things of apprehension. Or perhaps it is just that the human bones are after all simply bones in the ground, bones growing into the plants and earth again, where everything changes into everything else. David tells us that the root of one plant entered through the base of someone's skull and grew out through the orbit of an eye.

"You have to really slow down to do it," I say, watching Liz brushing and scraping away down in the grave. "You need to be patient."

"Yes. I haven't done this for thirty years and I'm feeling really good. Peaceful."

"I suppose you have to just slow down and respond to whatever turns up."

"Yes, that's what it is."

To David she says, "Some bits of blanket around here."

"Any buttons?" Michael asks.

"It seems they were just wrapped in blankets."

It is hot and the wind is blowing dust and bits of garbage around. My back hurts and I want to get out of the sun. I notice that the archaeologists have fold-up chairs, a hat and sunblock, a Thermos for lunch, and a cellphone. There is heat and wind and dust and cold. There is digging, brushing away, measuring, sorting, talking to the media, writing up, addressing community meetings, answering the questions of the curious public like ourselves, forming the treasure of silent bones and stones and things into stories and dioramas, collecting up ancestors, making up a history, making a museum.

The more care you take, the better quality of information you can derive. David has said that in this excavation, which is both salvage and a kind of discovery, everything must be precisely documented. The skeletons, the roots, the copper ornaments, the earth and bits of sacking, the municipal diggers that ripped them out, and the formal excavation that followed. Perhaps, as the team work together in the face of these remains from the early diamond years, the ritual of taking care becomes a sort of reparation. As though it were possible to recover what has been lost, to fix what has been shattered.

HUMAN

It would appear that the common conception of evolution is that of
a competing species running a sort of race through time on planet
earth, all on the same running field, some dropping out, some flag-
ging, some victoriously in front. If the background and foreground
are reversed, and we look at it from the side of the "conditions" and
their creative possibilities, we can see these multitudes of interactions through hundreds of other eyes.

GARY SNYDER

The National Monuments sign says "early humans left vast numbers of stone artefacts between 1.2 and 0.7 million years ago". It
says they were early human beings, our kind, people not animals. But
when does an animal become a human being? How can one tell?

Having shown us his skeletons, David has given me directions to
some archaeological sites in the Kimberley region. We decide to begin
with Canteen Kopje, a location near the Vaal River. As the site of the
first alluvial diamond workings in South Africa in 1869, it is a place
where, as Mary Barber recounts, the diggers discovered very old stone
tools as well as other treasure. Since that time, with the exception of
one anomalous and seemingly ancient skull, possibly from sediments

closer to the river, archaeologists have not found significant human remains at the site. But what I have come to see is this: the source of diamonds and handaxes near the river, the confluence of many diggings, the buried stones that last forever, the multitude in the field.

As we're driving towards Barkly West the children begin to bicker and whine. We buy white rolls, cheese, tomatoes and cold drinks in the town and promise a picnic at the site. To get there we take a turn off the main road, then drive through a gate and up a gravelly track to park the car somewhere in the veld at an outdoor museum marked by a little display case of information, its thick glass shattered by vandals. I sit down on a concrete slab beside the broken glass to butter bread, hand out juice and biscuits. The day is hot, a small wind blowing, pale grasses moving in the heat.

One answer to the question about humans and animals is to say that some time around 2.5 million years ago our brains became bigger, our teeth smaller, and we learnt to make stone artefacts. Perhaps these were the deciding features that marked the change. As we look back from here to there, the arbitrary names take shape from scattered fossil bones to speak of the long slow wandering of human kinds across the unfathomable years. *Homo habilis, Homo rudolfensis, Homo ergaster, Homo erectus, Homo heidelbergensis, Homo helmei, Homo neanderthalensis, Homo sapiens . . .* Different kinds, different bones, family.

The genealogies that describe us are varied and full of conjecture and debate. Nobody really knows. Yet, while the story of the beings called *Homo* must always be provisional, it is a story of the ancestry that all living human beings inherit. In making the journey from home to this dry region, I think I hope to find some trace of that inheritance. Our skeletons will soon dissolve to earth and plant and everything else, and human fossil limbs are rare. But artefacts of stone retain the tracks of human habitation in the land. They do not decay like bones and things of wood and shell and leather. Like the diamonds that our present times will leave behind, they almost seem permanent, the scattered, buried things that our warm hands have made.

The oldest known hominid artefacts are called Oldowan. These are the sort of tools found in the Olduvai Gorge in Tanzania by Mary Leakey and her team, stone implements that people made for about a million years. They are quite rudimentary but more sophisticated than the hammering stones used by nut-cracking wild chimpanzees, although the similarities are intriguing. In South Africa, Oldowan tools have been dated to between 1.7 and 2 million years old.

The next kind of stone technology, or industry as archaeologists would call it, is what is known as the Acheulean, named after the hamlet of Saint-Acheul in Northern France, where handaxes of different ages were found in a series of river terraces. Acheulean artefacts are big and made with a recognisable sense of symmetry and design. These are the handaxes and cleavers dug up too in ploughed fields and suburban gardens in many parts of South Africa, and picked up around False Bay. The farmers whose ploughs unearthed them called the handaxes amandelklippe because of their shape. Technically they are known as bifaces, both sides flaked by striking pieces off a core with a hammerstone. Inconceivably, the same technology endured with minimal variation for more than a million years. During that time the handaxe and the cleaver travelled across the world from Africa to India and beyond: one transmission in all those generations, almond stone and cleaver.

In the late 1920s this long, long reach of human practice received a new name, the Earlier Stone Age. Breaking with previous classifications which had interpreted South African prehistory in terms of European models, the archaeologist John Goodwin initiated a locally based system of classification which described three major stages of development: the Earlier Stone Age, the Middle Stone Age and the Later Stone Age. In broad terms this model is still in use today, though recent finds might shift the datings back.

As the industry following Acheulean technology, the term "Middle Stone Age" refers to the period when, with a change in stone-working techniques and smaller, flaked tools beginning to replace the bifaces around 250 000 years ago, people became, anatomically at least, like modern human beings. Digging, collecting and sorting, archaeologists went on to name the diverse assemblages of so-called Middle Stone Age industries after the current names of locations where they were discovered, places like Howieson's Poort or Still Bay.

Closer then, much closer to ourselves, the Later Stone Age is said to have begun around 40 000-30 000 years ago. It flourished through the Holocene, the last 10 000 years, and lingered in smaller and smaller traces into the end of the nineteenth century, when //Kabbo and the others could yet tell stories to Wilhelm Bleek and Lucy Lloyd about hunting and gathering and the making of stone tools. This is the period associated unambiguously with rock art and pottery, ostrich eggshell beads and tortoiseshell bowls, bows and arrows and formal burial of the dead. Stone tools were generally smaller and more diverse, consisting of bladelets, arrowheads, scrapers and so on. Again the different industries were classified according to form and function, and named for the places where they were first found.

For many people now who are at all interested in prehistory, this latest period, with its diverse traces of story and culture and its continuities into present time, seems to be the most evocative and compelling. But for me the idea of the handaxes at Kathu began a sort of quest to apprehend the almond tools, and to imagine our subsequent technologies and cultural practice as inheritors of their craft, to see this present moment in the context of deep time.

After the diamond diggers at Canteen Kopje came the archaeologists, digging, sorting, labelling, counting. Picnicking now beside the vandalised information boards of the outdoor exhibit, we read that the site is a Stone Age treasure trove, with maybe a hundred million artefacts. What distinguishes it from an archaeological point of view is the hoard of such Acheulean tools and their great size. Certainly the cores are massive. It has been said about the site, and often repeated, that not only are there enough specimens to fill a museum to overflowing, but even to build it of them also.[31] The oldest levels of the digs unearthed some of the hugest handaxes ever found, and a photograph shows people holding what are said to be the heaviest-ever handaxe, which weighs 7.7 kilograms, and the longest, which is 38.5 centimetres.

After lunch we set out to follow the path around the kopje. Almost immediately Sophie starts moaning, "Do we have to *walk*? I've got thorns! Take off these socks!"

There are blackjacks and other scratchy seeds in her socks. Take them off, pick each one out.

"Look at these beautiful stones," Michael says, bending to the ground. "Look," he shows her, "they're banded agates and chalcedony."

But Sophie is not happy.

"Carry me!" she shouts plaintively.

She wants her mother. She wants me with her. Camel thorn, buffalo thorn, umbrella thorn, she does not like this scratchy, sweaty, dusty, rocky place, even if there are some pretty pebbles scattered about. Yes, my little child, my sweetheart. Here I am, far from home with a sore back and looking at stones, and all you want is to be held in my arms.

"Come on, be brave," I say, holding her close. "You're a strong girl. You can be tough. Just take my hand."

On either side of the dry path are great piles of rock left by various diggers. But where are all the artefacts?

"Look," Michael points, "a big handaxe, and here's another one, and here. You have to slow down to see them."

And then I see. A few are strangely sharp and unweathered, but many of the big worked rocks are now so old, the almond stones so old and worn that they are beginning to look like natural objects again. Slowing

down, I see the heaped-up piles of ancient tools, pale golden andesite
among the gravels. Whatever stratigraphy was once here, the quiet,
long layering of the years has been irrevocably overturned by digging. Heaped up as gravels and leavings from the diamond years and
the archaeological digs, many of the worked stone artefacts are really
big. Several have been painted white and used to mark the edge of
the path.

The tools at our feet are thought to be a million years old and more. A million years. How long is that? How can anyone imagine this depth of time? In Cape Town Duncan said to me that if you stand on Table Mountain it is about a kilometre down to sea level. So if the mountain could be filed away, a millimetre each year, that would be a million years. Having now driven to Kimberley we have thought of the distance, about a thousand kilometres, as a million metres. Imagined in this way, driving or walking here, each metre travelled could signify the passing of a year, and the journey from home in the city to this place, all the way back to this small hill, would be about a million years.

For a moment these metaphors convey a flash of vastness. And then the mind returns to incomprehension. I pick up a smaller handaxe from the pile, smoothed and almost fitting in my hand. The rock is warm from the sun. Hold it, grasp the old stone tool, imagine the hands that made and held this stone. Big hands. Human beings. Walk along the path together, holding the heavy almond rock in one hand and Sophie's small, warm hand in the other.

Suddenly Sky trips and falls into a patch of thorns. Crying, crying, he is desperate: "Mommy! Mommy!"

Michael scrapes the thorns off the palms of his hands with a pocket-knife. I sit down, slow down, hold my boy.

"When are we going home to the *puppy*?" Sophie is insistent.

"Okay now, listen," I say firmly. "You have to listen and you two have to make an effort. We've come all this way, and these are very special places. You have to let me see them. This is my work."

We stand up and continue, Sky's hand in mine this time. Walking on, we see piles and piles of worked rocks and stone tools on either side of the path. Cars roar past on the road to Barkly West. The factory on the hill puffs and hoots. Suddenly, a movement to the side of the path draws our attention.

"Look! A tortoise!"

Michael wanders on but the children come to sit on my lap to watch. Sit still, don't move, just look. The tortoise is huge, certainly heavier than I could lift. It stops to look at us with a beaky dinosaur face, the feet scaly, the claws long and sharp, the hard shell dusty. The gaze of tortoise looking at human beings and human beings looking back must be as old as the stone I hold in my hand. And this tortoise is alive in the stony thornveld, still here.

"Look," I say to Sophie and Sky, "it's as though he's saying to us, 'I'm still here.' There used to be so many animals around, buck and lions and elephants, all of them. There were hippos in the river too, and there would have been giraffes and wildebeest, everything. They're all gone now, or most of them, the big ones anyway. But here he is still, the tortoise, or maybe she. They've been here a long time, tortoises."

After the hunters and the farmers, the diamond diggers and the archaeologists, here this old slow gaze returns, enduring. Slowly the tortoise walks away from us to the cover of a bush.

A bush, a tree, some grass. Visiting as city people from another ecosystem, we see the scratchy thornveld as a wilderness of bushes, trees and grasses, their names uncertain, their lives and qualities unknown.

But not so long ago, at least within the reach of oral history, and for a long, long time before that, the same dry plants were medicine, story, food, and the veld was intimately inhabited. The grey-green camphor leaves helped asthma, chest complaints and toothache, the branches were burnt and the smoke inhaled for headaches, and the woolly flowers plucked by birds to line their nests. Buffalo thorn was good for boils and swollen glands, the fruits for beer. Umbrella thorn, the haak-en-steek, had pods and gum that were nutritious, the branches were a home for sociable weavers, and the roots held liquid that might quench your thirst in the desert. Camel thorn, the big iconic one, this tree beloved of giraffes, *Acacia erioloba*, had ear-lobe-shaped pods that were eaten by buck, with insects inhabiting the thorns, geckos and scorpions in the bark, sociable weavers building in the branches. There was blue bush or bloubos, the small berries delicious, the roots chewed after a meal to clear the palate and clean the teeth. And the tangled puzzle bush gave berries and flexible branches for chest pain and stomach pain and for making rain, the green twigs burning into smoke, rain clouds gathering.

These things are mostly now forgotten. I understand that there has been pressure in recent years to reopen Canteen Kopje for prospecting and to remove its status as a national monument. Through local negotiation and foreign funding, this pressure was apparently resisted, and the space within the fence protected from further excavation. But beyond that fence the diamond digging has begun again to shovel up the million-year-old record of inhabitation in the interests of other treasure.

At the culmination of the walk, a signpost innocently informs visitors that the expertise and wealth generated by innumerable diggings on the Diamond Fields were significant factors in the early industrialisation of South Africa.

Once the children have been returned to the car, I walk again to sit alone on a great pile of pale rocks. Many of them are the worn old almond stones cast aside by the diamond diggers, tools made with a hammerstone perhaps a million years ago. In all that time the course of the river we call the Vaal has changed a little, but still it flows.

I continue to wonder what they were like, our ancestors. The size of the tools and the few fossil remains found elsewhere in the world suggest that our Acheulean forebears were bulkier than we are now, with powerful arms and legs, big human beings, who made big tools. From the scattering of their tools near pans, vleis, wetlands and river banks, it seems that they liked to live near water. So this neighbourhood near the river must have been a good place to be. Stone, kopje, river, people, many years, breathing in and breathing out, and the sound of the river never too far away.

Human animals, animal persons, what was our original face before our mothers gave birth to us? Sitting still in this place, sitting down in the place of old worked stones beside the river, what can we know? It is dry up at the site, dusty and full of stones. Beyond and below is the river and the river flows onward, heart of river people flowing in fish and crocodile and hippopotamus, hard stones flaked to make a tool.

And here at the beginning is the sound of water, heart of river flow-ing, here. Sitting still on the heaped stone tools of deep old time, cars pass on the road, a factory drones on the hill, the warm breath moves, evanescent things.

Homo heidelbergensis, Australopithecus africanus, how far back? Moth-ers, fathers, children, teachers – we sit down here alone and together with everyone who has inhabited this place before us. The warm breath moves from mother to child and on, each small body curled in the womb, each cry, each life, each death. Our blood is red, our blood flows onwards, warm heart beating, breathing still. In the course of this river, there is only one seat. This place, now. There is only one breath, this inhalation and exhalation, a brief warm breath, this thread of breath, our breath, a million years and more. The smooth, old handaxe rests in my hand. Put it back among the others. Let it go.

Returning along the path, the sudden smell of grasses opens in the sun. Sweet, lively, unmistakeable, the fragrance of grasses of the savan-nah reaches to us now across uncountable generations. As simple and prolific as grass, these grasses endure. Sweet trace on the breeze, this smell, remembering.

And then it is gone.

ANIMALS

We should resist the temptation to assume that since stories are stories they are, in some sense, unreal or untrue, for this is to suppose that the only real reality, or true truth, is one in which we, as living, experiencing beings, can have no part at all. Telling a story is not like weaving a tapestry to *cover up the world*, it is rather a way of guiding the attention of listeners or readers *into* it.

TIM INGOLD

Sitting at the yellow Formica table in the little kitchen at Gum Tree Lodge, I can hear Sky in the next room charging Sophie two cents a ride to take her soft animals up the cable car to the top of the bunk bed. She has brought some coppers for our trip and doesn't mind paying. After all, for the twins there is no question about it: animals are people, fascinating ones.

When my mother called from Cape Town and asked Sophie about our trip, I heard her answering, "Granny, there's a puppy here, such a sweet puppy. And you know, the puppy's mommy isn't a dog, she's a person. He was taken away from his dog mommy and now his mommy is a person. He sleeps in the bed with his mommy at night. He's got pyjamas with stars and moons, and he's such a sweet puppy. I kissed him on the nose."

Sophie herself is the mother of many animals. She does not like dolls but makes clothes for all her children, gives them birthday parties and picnics and puts them to bed. Sky's big bear is also a person, a magical being who can fly and change shape and pick up mountains. Now, having survived the car journey, the family of animal children are experiencing a holiday in Kimberley.

I wonder how much longer these animal stories will last. It is said that there was a time when animals were people, and people were animals. There was a time when people were springbok and they really cried, a time when lions and leopards could talk. If I say that for our children, perhaps all children, that time is now, does this mean that it is childishness to tell such stories?

Wildebeest Kuil Rock Art Centre, not far from Kimberley, is a place engraved with many animals. On our arrival at the small modern visitors' centre, we meet a young man with dreadlocks, dressed in cool Joburg style and working at a computer. He is not wearing a loincloth, he does not look particularly poor, and he is not engaged in hunting or tracking.

"Is he a Bushman?" Sophie asks, pointing.

"Sh! Don't talk about people."

"Why not?"

"Just because."

A poster notes that "the colonial experience was devastating for San people" but that Wildebeest Kuil is an important rock art site. We pay the entrance fee to the young man, feed the children some chocolate digestive biscuits and wander together towards the patch of engraved rocks on a small hill in a wide reach of grassland.

The earth is red, the grasses pale and green. A light wind is blowing, hawks hovering. Walking among grasses and stones, we pass some red termite heaps. I remember that in the /Xam narratives the eggs are called Bushman rice, a delicacy that was scooped, gathered and stored.

In one of the stories a girl is crying at night because she wants to eat Bushman rice. Her crying wakes a lion who comes to carry off her parents. Stories about lions are numerous in the collection – tales of danger, respect, confrontation and sometimes even magical power, tales that caution against speaking the name of the lion, and tales of particular people's encounters, like the one Dia!kwain told about a lion who acquired a taste for a certain young man after licking his tears.[32] But in this unusual story, from Dia!kwain's sister !Kweiten-ta-//ken, the lion is killed by the quick-thinking young girl. She sets fire to his hair, and he runs away and dies. Her mother praises her warmly, and says that her reward will indeed be the termites' eggs that she wants. She says to her daughter, "We will break for thee a Bushman rice's ostrich eggshell for thou didst keep us alive."[33] In other stories, the termites are rain's things, creatures that appear to the world after the rain.

From somewhere in the veld a tall man walks out to meet us. He has a wry, lively face and is wearing a soft, loose-fitting Mandela-type shirt.

His name is Salvador – Batista Salvador – and he comes from Angola.

Again Sophie is uncertain. "Is he really a Bushman?"

I ask him what he feels about these names: "Bushman, San, what should we say?"

"I don't mind about those names," he says. "They're okay. Our people are the !Xun and Khwe."

Batista walks ahead up the small hill to a discreet boardwalk that leads among the engraved rocks. From a short distance they look like scattered stones, reddish brown. Coming closer, we can recognise the animals, pale, soft-edged forms that gleam out of the dark. A delicate elephant, a rhinoceros, a hartebeest, an ostrich, many eland, a few human beings, some grids and gateways and a burst of sun. The rock is andesite, the outer crust weathered darker so that when this layer is chipped away the lighter stone is revealed within, and the tenderly observed bodies of animals emerge against the dark. But why are they here on the rocks on the hill, animals and people? Rain's thing, perhaps, this phrase from the Bleek-Lloyd Archive for animals connected with the making of rain. Perhaps they are images of healing, memories of the trance. Or a hunting diary. Or an instruction manual about the local veld. It is dry here now, but after good rains there would be water in the small kuil below the hill, water for the animals and people who would have come here for ever to drink. The engravings at Wildebeest Kuil are thought to be between a thousand and two thousand years old, Later Stone Age. But the scattered stone tools go all the way back to the people who were here in the Acheulean period.

In the very last years of this long inhabitation, the land passed by various means of trickery and blood from indigenous peoples into the hands of white farmers. It is not known exactly who was killed when they fought to hold this territory. But certainly there were missionaries in the region as well as settlers who killed Bosjesmans. And although Khoe-San rebels defied them both, by the 1870s Wildebeest Kuil was in the firm possession of a farmer, one Dirk Bredenkamp. The local people who remained became his labourers.

By then this part of the country had become interesting to history and trade because of diamonds. Although none were found on the farm, it was a convenient stopping point for a journey between the alluvial diggings at sites like Canteen Kopje and the mine at Kimberley, and the place became for a while a halfway house hotel. The eland, the elephant, the hartebeest and the rhinoceros were all shot out, their home veld grazed by cattle and sheep and visited by diggers. Now standing among the rocks, you can still see far, far away in all directions across the flat wide veld. Smoky haze of Kimberley, cars on the road to Barkly West, distant green of thornveld trees at the rim of the savannah.

"This one's a gemsbok," Batista says. "It's one of the toughest animals, very powerful. It takes six to eight hours before you can tire it out. It doesn't need water like the others, so it's difficult to run it down."

"And this one? It looks like a sun."

"Yes, the geometric designs are used to draw power. It's like the animal ones, for the trance. We use the engravings to draw power from the animals, so that our body becomes hot. If you don't have the power, you won't last long in the trance, you'll be exhausted after only three hours."

He faces us with his whole body, senses open, lively. "In the trance I need the power to see into your body, to see what needs to be healed, so that I can draw the arrows of sickness out."

I wonder then what it is that needs to heal, and how the arrows will be extracted.

"You're saying 'we' about the engravings. What do you mean?"

"It's the same. Our people don't do rock art. We carve wood. But it's the same."

Batista's people are a group of San from Angola. Although their language and history are different from that of the last San inhabitants of this region, they now own the land at Wildebeest Kuil and are involved in managing the site. Their recent story begins with the Angolan War.

Disaffected with their treatment by the Popular Movement for the Liberation of Angola, many of the San who had fled to Namibia joined the South African Defence Force as trackers and fighters. They are said to have been feared by the enemy for their skill and bravery. When Namibia gained independence in 1990 and SWAPO won the election, the SADF brought around seven thousand !Xun and Khwe men, women and children to South Africa to live at a military base called Schmidtsdrift. They were given tents and promised houses within six months. But no houses were ever built and it was a miserable environment for anyone to live in. Then, in 1996, the diverse group put together the

money they had received from the government's land restitution pro-
gramme and bought the land around and including Wildebeest Kuil.
Since then members of the community have made art and crafts for sale
at the site, others have been involved with the Northern Cape Rock
Art Trust in developing and managing the site in association with the
McGregor Museum, and a few people have been trained by the Wits
Rock Art Research Institute as guides to the engravings. At the visitors'
centre it says that "the !Xun and Khwe see in the art a link to a broad
Khoisan cultural inheritance in South Africa".

"You feel a connection with the engravings?" I ask.

"Yes."

The quiet rocks are peopled with elephants and buck and human
beings, clear good lines and fine attention. Ignoring the official tour
guide text prepared by the McGregor Museum, Salvador continues to
speak of the trance, of people becoming animals and magical beings, of
people bending over as they dance, or flying to another place with the
spirit. For a moment he shows us what this looks like, bending forward, taking little steps, his arms stretched up and back behind his
head like wings.

"It's really dangerous," he says. "If you stay away too long, you can't
come back. Sometimes the young ones just don't make it."

I find myself appealing to him as an authority on recent history:
"Batista, why do you think the local San, the /Xam and others, disappeared so quickly? We know they were hunted and killed, but why was
it so successful?"

"Because they lost their land. When you lose your land, you lose everything."

Perhaps if a community possesses no abstract Word, no precious books to carry with it, and if a people's stories, pictures and language inhabit a particular environment in the intimate detail that hunting and gathering require, then the loss of home must surely be irrevocable.

"You see," Batista continues, "the eland is very special for all San. Once the eland is gone, the people get sick. We didn't see it, we didn't know we were doing it. But when the animals are gone, the people are gone forever."

His face is sad and wry. I believe him. I also wonder about questions of authenticity. What he is saying recalls interpretations of San culture and belief that have been influential in the study of rock art, and I wonder how much of this way of seeing he has learnt from the university specialists – a San culture that endures across regions and generations, people of the eland, people of the trance. His own experience and that of the !Xun and Khwe would seem likely to be more complex, mixed-up, fractured and strange than such ideas would suggest. Or was the Fall really so recent, and life here before colonial history simply aeons of long time passing, of people and animals together in this place, animals who were once people, people who were once animals?

Yet sitting among the engraved rocks on the little hill, I know this must be where people have sat for hundreds of thousands of years. Sitting here and watching, wind moving the grasses, hawk soaring overhead, animals out there on the plain. Sitting here, they could have

seen the springbok in their multitudes and the steenbok, gemsbok, blesbok, kudu, eland, zebra and wildebeest. There were lions and elephants
in the veld, jackals, wild dogs, hyenas, caracal cats, hares and porcupines, probably rhino and giraffe.

Now there are San crafts on sale in London and at Disneyland, and
Coca-Cola here at Wildebeest Kuil. The deplaced, displaced *Homo sapiens* seem everywhere and nowhere, pushing onwards into the future.
Perhaps it is not surprising if the animals engraved in the rocks, or the
stories of place and animal persons in the Bleek-Lloyd Collection, should
become for some contemporary humans, perhaps even for Batista himself, a kind of sacred text – like a precious stone, like water in the desert,
like a refuge in the winds of forgetting.

Batista continues, "The last Korana leader, he had a /Xam mother.
He said, 'When you see somebody who doesn't belong to your tribe,

never in the future let them have your land.' And Dia!kwain, he said the same thing, he said . . ."

And then Batista speaks in a beautiful language of clicking sounds that we cannot understand. Afterwards he translates: "It means when you go out to hunt and you see strange spoor on the land, you know you must move on."

Like many people with an opinion on rock art, Batista quotes the Bleek-Lloyd Archive, or at least an idea of it. At Wildebeest Kuil this reference evokes a rather particular history. While many of the Victorian visitors to the region in the late nineteenth century seem to have been seeking profit related to its mineral treasure, at least one man recorded the value of something beyond the accumulation of property, diamonds or livestock. In the early 1870s George William Stow made copies of the rock engravings at Wildebeest Kuil and sent them as part of a sizeable batch of so-called cartoons, rubbings and sketches of Bushman paintings and engravings to Wilhelm Bleek and Lucy Lloyd in Cape Town, who had recently begun recording the /Xam narratives. Bleek responded enthusiastically: "They are of the greatest possible interest," he wrote, "and evince an infinitely higher taste, and a far greater artistic faculty, than our liveliest imagination could have anticipated, even after having heard several glowing descriptions of them from eye-witnesses." He went on to suggest that their publication "cannot but effect a radical change in the ideas generally entertained with regard to Bushmen and their mental condition".[34] Whatever Bleek might have meant by this, within about a hundred years, in a sort of reciprocal loop, interpretations of the Bleek-Lloyd Archive by scholars such as Patricia Vinnicombe and David Lewis-Williams were to change significantly the study of rock art in South Africa and beyond.[35] In the period that followed, the engravings at Wildebeest Kuil continued to be of interest, and in 2000, when the Rock Art Research Institute at Wits University was approached by the Department of Environmental Affairs and Tourism to design a strategy to make South Africa the world's leading rock art tourism destination, this site was one of two selected for an injection of government funding. I understand that Batista was a member of a group who attended a course on rock art interpretation in the Drakensberg, organised by Wits. With such layers of recent involvement accumulating at the site, it is not surprising if what he has to say about the engravings should bear the traces of a range of stories.

Watching us now, his face is kind, earnest and amused. He says, "When I was in Amazon, it was the same. Siberia too. Always the same story. They come and take our land."

"It's always the same story, yes. But what were you doing in the Amazon? Part of an indigenous people's network?"

"Yes. I wanted to see what the Amazon people were doing, if it was like us. It's more or less the same. They use different poisons, but it's about seventy per cent the same as us."

The mention of poison reminds me of the time I came upon a puff adder lying in our path in the veld. Sophie nearly stepped on it, and we were all startled. I ask Batista how poison is extracted for the arrows.

He says, "You hold him behind the head, here. If he bites your hand, you must hold the arm tight above the place, like this. Your friend must make a knife red-hot in the fire, and then you cut. Suck the poison out. The snake, he watches you. You must stay absolutely still. When you move too soon, he says, 'Yes, that's what I was waiting for,' and he comes after you."

"How do you know all this about animals and hunting?" I ask.

"My uncle. He was getting old, so he told me things. Do you know that the best hunters are not lions but wild dogs? The lions think and try to calculate what to do, but the dogs work together. They do it together, roll them over. When my uncle took me hunting, he said, 'You must listen, just listen.' So I listened. You can hear the kudu say: 'Hmmph.' You must sit the whole day and learn to listen, watch how the animals are moving and eating. Watch them. From their skills we learn our skills. They can tell you things too. If the birds are making a lot of noise, they may be telling you about a big snake, or a dangerous animal. Animals are also our friends. You need to listen."

Listening to him speak, we glimpse for a moment the animals he sees. Their mind is keen, their point of view exact. They look at us. The world is watching.

I ask him if I can take a photograph, and where he would like to sit. He finds a rock where he will be surrounded by his favourite engravings.

"It's a church for me, here," he says. "I don't need to go to church. I just come and sit over here on my own."

To describe the site as being like a church could be an echo of rock-art scholars like David Lewis-Williams. Or a way of finding a metaphor in English for the resonance of the place. Or neither, or both.

"Yes," I say, "it's a powerful place. You can feel it."

Batista says, "If you have a problem, maybe with your marriage, you come and sit here in these places and ask the ancestors. Ask them if this marriage is going to work. They will speak to you in a dream soon afterwards. They will tell you what to do, the ancestors."

His face becomes grave. "But these days the younger generations are not interested in the old knowledge. They are being resettled from Schmidtsdrift now, just over there at Platfontein, too close to the city, too close to Kimberley. Have you ever heard of a Bushman living so close to the city?"

I suppose this is what is called promoting the stereotype. While I am thinking of how to respond, he answers his own question: "There's going to be violence, rape, all these things."

Sophie and Sky have been sitting a little distance away in the veld, banging stones together, pretending they are tools. When they join us, Salvador starts talking about his own son, who is always collecting snakes and scorpions. He is quite big now, he says, but when he was a baby his grandfather marked him as a possible shaman.

"Maybe one day your children will become a shaman too," he continues. "They will need to choose one of the three: rainmaker, healer, or the one who calls the animals. The first two are the most difficult, most painful. You have to be able to hold the pain in your body so you can take it away from other people. It's very difficult."

Back at the information centre Batista puts on a video about the San for us to watch. Afterwards we meet his young wife, sitting on a plastic chair and doing a clapping song with a year-old toddler, their youngest child. The cheerful baby walks towards us on unsteady legs, and I sit down on the tiled floor and put out my arms. She takes my hands and smiles, then walks to Sophie and Sky and hugs them. In the background the men are still talking.

Salvador is saying, "I want a museum that shows the genocide. Not for children or sensitive people, but I do want people to know. Did you know there was a bounty of ten shillings on the head of San leaders? I want people to know what happened."

We buy a wire car for Sky, a bracelet for Sophie and a book about engravings for me. Michael gives Batista his own pocketknife as a present for the older son he mentioned, the one who likes collecting snakes. Batista is interested in the tool, inspects the blade with care.

As we are leaving, Michael asks whether he has heard about the current predictions for climate change, that most of the western part of the country is likely to be desertified within the lifetime of our children. Batista shrugs, shakes his head.

"I suppose it'll be good for people who know how to live in the desert," Michael says.

Salvador nods, smiles.

We smile too, clasp hands. "Goodbye, thank you."

He bows slightly and turns away, more tourists waiting.

Sophie asks again, "But *was* he a Bushman?"

"Yes," we say, "he is."[36]

Later David Morris tells me that Batista's gemsbok is really an eland, and that our visit to the site was meant to have been differently narrated. We were supposed to have seen a different video, and observed the engravings in relation to the taped audio-tour's account of recent and ancient history, along with some beautiful stories from the Bleek-Lloyd Archive, stories about rainmaking and the cutting of the rain animal which walked the land on rain's legs, stories about male and female rain, about /Kaggen and eland, stories that are like the wind, that float along to another place.

In retrospect, for all the work that various people have put into it, perhaps we were lucky to miss the official version. Whatever Batista says about the engravings must to some extent reflect what he learnt from the rock-art specialists. But his stories are also more than this. Equipped with a variety of ancient and modern tools, his mind seems playful and sensitive, reaching to perform the stories of the place for strangers from the city like ourselves. Is what he says authentic? Is it true? The questions speak of a longing that cannot be fulfilled, a visitor's wish to meet in him or at least in his story some veritable other, a longing for a tradition that is uncontaminated, for the true trace of a world of hunter-gatherers before it all went wrong. More likely, Batista Salvador of Angola, Namibia, Schmidtsdrift, Wildebeest Kuil and elsewhere is a modern human being much like ourselves, a person wandering between worlds.

He told us that he had bought springbok and eland to graze in the veld across the road, and I wonder how this could be. Perhaps he knows this is what we would like to hear, or what he would like to believe. Perhaps all his stories are all story: fabrication and desire. Yet Batista's words and gestures engage our attention powerfully, and we remember them. His words are a kind of performance enacted with grace and humour, a taste of something light and wise, a sort of theatre. The look in his eyes as he speaks seems detached, imaginative, ironic, gazing among the rocks to a place where the land is still inhabited by elephants and buck and human beings, where animals are people and people are animals. His stories of them reach to us across the worlds. Perhaps he too seeks refuge from forgetting.

As we drive away from Wildebeest Kuil, the children begin saying that they are really hungry again and they want to go home to the puppy. We feed them more chocolate digestives and some sandwiches and tell them there is still one more site, the glacial pavements at Nooitgedacht. A few more engravings. Off the main road, not far from Wildebeest Kuil, we pass an abandoned stone house and stop the car.

"Listen to the place," I say. "It's quiet."

For the first time on this expedition there is no sound or sight of cars or other people. There is no guide and no information. Walking towards the site, the twins meet a long line of big ants carrying seeds and flowers. Sky follows them to their home and discovers a pile of discarded husks outside the door.

Settling down on the ground beside them he calls to us, "I just love looking at these ants."

Beyond the ants, downhill where the river used to flow, the rock is big: a wide expanse of smooth grey. Across the surface, marks of the moranic till sweep in great slow lines, long tracks of the stones and rubble carried along by the glacier 300 million years ago. Ice and rocks move slowly, mountains and waters flow, and the land is older than it is possible for us to grasp. Inscribed against this great reach of time, the human tracks engraved on the rock are all so young: the outlined head of a giraffe, a buck, concentric circles, grids and gateways, light marks on stone.

"Look!" Sophie says, finding a pattern. "Another spiral."

She has been seeing spirals all around Kimberley. In the pressed-iron ceilings of the Mine Museum, in the plastic broekielace at Gum Tree Lodge, in the design of the bedroom curtains and the rattling spiralling seed pods of camel-thorn trees. We remember the waves at home and the shells and the ferns.

Finding things now without a guide, the children crawl over the great warm rock in a quiet dream, fingers following the patterns. Lying on the rock, our bodies breathe the midday stillness, imagine the glacier and the slow sweep of stones, imagine other people bending to engrave the pattern, people talking here and wondering, healing and mourning and telling stories, the things we human animals do.

The day is quiet. It is warm on the wide grey rock, no clouds or cars. The veld beyond holds traces of those who still live here. Dung and feathers, little footprints, bones and quills, a myriad lives.

PATTERN

Do not think flowing is like wind and rain moving from east to west.
The entire world is not unchangeable, is not immovable. It flows.
Flowing is like spring. Spring with all its numerous aspects is
called flowing. When spring flows there is nothing outside of spring.

DŌGEN

At Gum Tree Lodge the lawns are watered every day. There are yellow chrysanthemums growing in the garden, painted swings and a jungle gym and a hoopoe in the tree. That is in front. At the back, the yards run untended into dusty stones and thorn trees.

"Come, I want to show you," Michael says. "Wherever you look here in the veld there's garbage."

Plastic bags and bits of pipe, an old shoe, some rubber, barbed wire, wood, a rusty spring. All useless broken things have turned up here among the grass and stones. Away. Throw it away. The puppy's mommy walks to the edge of her garden and tosses something out as far as she can into the veld. Away. Some day archaeologists may be grateful.

Walking out beyond the yards we find an open pit that has been dug for dumping waste and rubble. Looking in, the edge reveals the hidden strata of the land, rippling flow of shale and earth, layer on layer, here unseen beneath our feet.

"I wanted to show you that as well," Michael says. "Look at the flow in the rock, the different colours. That would be something: an artwork, just digging an open pit to reveal the unseen flow. Just that."

The children find a mousebird's tail feather and pieces of broken wood. They will use them for making a little boat to float on the river.

The river is a small one, the Riet. David Morris has offered to take us there to see Driekopseiland, a place marked with a multitude of engravings which he has spent many years researching.

"How are the skeletons going?" we ask when he meets us at the museum.

"Slowly. We now think they're earlier than the Flu Epidemic of 1918. The Siege of Kimberley is a possibility. That's 1900. But it's starting to look as though they may be connected with the mines. De Beers have uncovered something from their records. There was a fire disaster in 1888. They may have to confront some history."

Driving out, we talk about early Kimberley, where his great-great-grandfather and Michael's great-grandfather both owned digging claims in the 1870s. They probably knew each other, both of them engineers, those men with their moustaches. David tells us that a later ancestor of his had the lemon trees planted along the city streets.

"I think Kimberley is where it started, apartheid," he says. "Things could have taken a different turn, but here there was a change of scale.

Segregation was more institutionalised, and so labour migrancy, coming to work and going again, became a system. During the Siege, they built a circle of forts and redoubts, and black settlements that were outside were cleared, and people consolidated in designated 'locations'. For most people here, urban segregation was a fact long before the 1923 Act."

History, mining, archaeology. We share an interest in the digging up of buried things, of things forgotten and thrown away, of places marked with habitation, and in the stories of this treasure. Driving off the main road through old wire gates and onto farm roads, David tells us about his work on the engravings. We talk about smoke and blood and water in the Bleek-Lloyd Collection, and the significance of flowing things, of things that change. We drive past mealie fields, row upon row of dry-looking mealies planted in grids of monoculture parallel to the road. At intervals we see great conical piles of white powder, snowy white peaks. Like the breasts of young girls, Michael says.

David explains, "It's fertiliser. Gets into the water. It's affecting the farms downstream, and even the agriculturalists are worried that it's not sustainable. You'll see at the site how the alien plants are clogging things up. Too much fertiliser. We don't know what it's doing to the engravings."

Approaching the river from a distance along the dusty farm road, you see dry grass and gumtrees and the flat backs of the grey rocks in the river, what geologists call glaciated andesite basement rock, cracked and marked by the slow tracks of the ancient ice. Looking closer, you realise that the hide of the rock is covered all over with human designs. Each mark is different, yet the outlined forms are similarly drawn, more than 3 500 engravings chipped out of the stone using a sharp stone point, the worked patterns showing lighter against the grey. Nearly all are what are called "geometric" – not obviously representational, yet no straight ruled lines.

Walking across the sea of patterns, we spread out on the grey expanse, bending to touch the radiating lines that snake and wander like the tracks of termites in wood, the path of a creature in the sand, a map of meandering trails. The wandering lines connect to circles, wheels and suns chipped out of the stone, to grids and gateways, human tracks that repeat and repeat, never the same, walking on the body of the rock.

It is believed that people have been coming to Driekopseiland to engrave the rocks from possibly more than two thousand years ago until the early nineteenth century. Since then, travellers, artists and archaeologists have offered various explanations as to their meaning and origin. David's key insight is that the engravings are inextricably part of a *place*, this place. The site, like other sites, is really an environment, not a collection of artefacts. Here, as elsewhere, the stone on which images are engraved or painted is never a neutral surface. At Klipfontein, he says, you can see this clearly in the engraving of a flamingo in the side of a hollowed rock. The specific placement is clearly deliberate in that the head of the flamingo is bent low towards the part of the rock where the rainwater collects, as though it is feeding.[37] Here at

Driekopseiland, the patterns on the rock are patterns that appear and disappear as the river floods and dries. Some of the engravings are below the current low-water mark, which means that the river must in the past have tended to dry up completely, revealing the vast rock from bank to bank. Other times, in the wet season, the river rises to cover it entirely. The patterns participate in this seasonal transformation. So their meaning is emplaced, as they say, in these changes, emerging and submerging as the waters fall and rise.

"One of the big disasters was the canal," David says. "The farmers wanted more water, so they built a canal from the Orange River. Before that, this river was seasonal. Now it flows perpetually. It's a crucial difference. More exotic trees (gumtrees) because there's more silt and moisture, and of course there's an impact on the engravings. The place is different now. Some of them are submerged all year. And if there's meaning in the ebb and flow, then their meaning's changed too."

"What about the weir?" I ask. Just above where we are standing, the water roars over a noisy weir that has been built across the river.

"That too, that was the start. The farmers wanted it, back in the forties, so they built right across some of the engravings. It could have been worse. I suppose many people just don't see what's here. You know, I came here one day in the 1980s and found some of the police washing their van with a bucket right over there on the engravings. There was a big yellow police van parked near the weir for a leisurely afternoon of washing and basking. I said to them, 'You should arrest yourselves!' I don't think it made much impression. They probably laughed. And then there was the time the farmer's son drove a grader over the engravings. You can see the bruised rocks over here."

As the sun climbs higher, some of the patterns, particularly the older or more abraded ones, seem to recede into the body of the rock. We ask what is the best time of day to see them clearly.

"It's best at dawn and at dusk, when the light is changing and the shadows are long. The contrasts show up well then. Dawn is better, actually. Those gumtrees block the sunset now."

I have read David's thesis about Driekopseiland and enjoyed the relation between his scholarly caution and the flowing river, between the precision of archaeological analysis and these meandering lines, between the rigours of the discipline and the fluid, visceral things with which the thesis is concerned. His subject, approached with the rigour of an academic voice, is this strange site. He calls it a powerful place, this place of the rock which he imagines might in some magical way embody the idea of water itself, !Khwa, the Great Water Snake, which lives in the river, here in this precious liminal realm that ebbs and flows. Beyond this, drawing on contemporary ethnographies and connections in Khoe-San thought between the menstruating girl and !Khwa, David thinks it possible that young women may have come to this place at the river after the period of seclusion that defined their first menstruation to be splashed by the water and make their mark on the rock. The old women would have splashed them.

The new maiden, as she is called in some of the Bleek-Lloyd narratives, stands in that powerful place between the hearth and the wild, between culture and nature. And here where we now stand are the marks of changing, of young girls at the threshold of fertility, here in this place at the river, the marks of the rites of blood and flow.

Dia!kwain called the new maiden "the rain's magic power". His sister !Kweiten-ta-//ken, who spent a short time in Mowbray in 1874 with her children, also described her in stories to Lucy Lloyd.[38] Sometimes, she says, her power is dangerous. She kills the water's children that are beautiful and striped, and she eats them in secret. Because of this, the whirlwind carries her and her family into the spring, and they are turned into frogs. At other times she is beneficent, painting the spring with the power of her new blood, painting with //ka or red ochre that it may not dry up, painting the young men like zebras to protect them from the destructive effects of the rain:

> The maiden, she ornaments the spring with //ka, when she becomes a maiden; she wishes that the spring may not dry up (lit. go out); because she wishes that the water might remain quietly in the spring. Because she wishes that the water may not dry up; that the water may remain in the spring. Therefore, they adorn the spring when they become maidens. Therefore they adorn the spring on account of it; therefore it is that they adorn the spring, on account of it; because they wish that the spring may not dry up, that it (the water) might remain quietly on account of it. Therefore the old women tell them about it; therefore they (the maidens) adorn the water's springs, on account of it. They wish

that the spring may not become dry. Hence it is, that the girls adorn the young men with stripes made of the //ka like a zebra, because they wish that the rain may not lightning kill them (the young men). Therefore, they (the maidens) adorn the young men, on account of it, for the rain comes out (in) the young men as sores.[39]

Walking now on the dry back of the Water Snake, the rock which holds the trace of slow glacier flow and the seasonal path of the river, this body which emerges and submerges in drought and flood, our feet touch stars and suns, stars within suns. Perhaps they are images that the mind sees in trance, or the stars within the darkness of the visual field. Perhaps they are the real heavenly bodies whose stories appear again and again in the marbled notebooks, stories of brightness and longing in which the idea of personhood wanders about among talking stars and talking flowers, people and animals.

Dia!kwain said to Lucy Lloyd, in her translation, "The stars are also things which resemble the moon; for they used formerly to be a person. Therefore, the star formerly sang of its elder sister; while it sang asking the time at which the //garaken flower should open." He goes on to tell her how the star sings to the flower, how someone else sings to the star, delighting in its beauty, and how the star is asking when the flower will open. Then he tells her of a song that is sung by the star, and especially by Bushmen women. "For the star," he says, "was once a child."[40]

"Yes," David says, "but when we read these words now, we think of the stars as being far away. In those stories I think the stars were here, immediately with us, and the spirit world too. These things were close."

"Perhaps," I say, "if stars can be persons and people can be animals, then nature isn't out there, it isn't separate."

If ideas of nature are always full of culture and full of the particular environments in which people live, then a hunter-gatherer's understanding of animals and plants must be quite different from the conceptual segregation of nature and culture that we industrialised people inherit. David points out that hunting-foraging San people would have seen what we call the natural environment in a variety of ways, depending on context. There are times, he says, when an animal is simply an other: game to be observed, analysed and tracked, meat to be butchered, cooked, eaten and so on. But then, in order to hunt well, a man must identify closely with his eland, feel the tremor of the springbok coming, sense in his body the living intelligence of the world. And in the healing dance, it is said that the threshold of animal and human dissolves and people become animals, dancing through the realms.

Strange, perhaps, standing on the rocks and talking about these things. And yet not strange. I feel as though we know each other well. He is about my age, and the inflections of accent, dress and gesture speak of growing up in similar times and places.

I say that I think what appeals to us now about these stories is not just to do with nostalgia or guilt, or wanting to romanticise an idea of "the San". Modernised people like ourselves could do with some new myths about nature and human agency. Perhaps we hope the stories about hunting and gathering might help us conceive ways of relating to the earth and to one another that are less dualistic, more sustainable and kind.

We talk about the North American writer Gary Snyder who has influenced my thinking on these things, his lifelong practice of what he calls writing the wild, writing in ordinary terms of the living world in which we participate, beyond and before all dualisms, inextricably.

Trying to articulate what seems to me the basic insight, I say: "As I see it, the point is really that the nature/culture divide that people talk about . . . it's not some wall that needs to be bashed down. It's not even permeable. The point is, it isn't really there. This is one system."

"Exactly," David says. "It isn't really there."

We speak about people who may be animals and stars, and people whose stories describe a living universe where everything changes. Honey may be masculine or feminine, thick and hard or soft and liquid. Fat, too, is like this, and water and rain. Smoke dissolves into air, the wind moves and settles, and the desert whirlwinds bring the spiralling red dust of the ancestors into our midst. Everything changes into everything else.

"Even words and stories are like this," David says. "Remember what //Kabbo said about stories. It's a beautiful image, that stories are like the wind, floating away to another place."

When //Kabbo used this image to Lucy Lloyd in 1873, he was speaking of home and his longing to return. Among other things, his homesickness describes a need for stories – growing restless in the Mowbray house, he wanted to be with his own people and to listen to them tell the stories of the place.[41] Remembering these words now, I imagine a point of view from which stories and metaphors are real as we are, present and evanescent, like everything else. I imagine a world not of things and entities, but seen with a precise and delicate understanding of how things change. Girls change into women, boys into men. First bleeding, first kill, these moments of transition. All things are made of flow and change, both people and other animals, wind and smoke, the changing river and the rocks.

Lower down, the river runs more swiftly, and you no longer hear or see the weir. This is the oldest part, where the engravings are more abraded, returning to the patterns of stone.

"It's wonderful here."

"Yes, I like this part of the site," David says. "We should take our shoes off, to feel the place in another dimension."

All shoes off, we sit together in quietness, no words left, just people sitting together on the great curved back of the Water Snake, grey rock marked by the slow walk of glacier and the brief patterns of human life. At the edge of the water the children are playing.

"Come and put your feet in," Sophie calls me.

It's cold. I stand with her, ankle-deep, holding hands at the sunlit edge where the water makes ripples against the rock, ripples of light and shade.

And then I see it, the pattern.

The pattern is the ripple of sand and the crests and troughs of tiny waves reflected on stone. Sun shines through, ripple of wave. This flowing. Holding hands with my daughter, feet wet at the edge of the rock, seeing what they saw: this radiating river flow, this sunlight making shadows, repeating and repeating, never the same. Here they came before us, here to this place in the river where one small stone makes circles, rippling outwards, and the little waves make patterns on the rock. Awakened to the flowing of blood and water, this may be the place where a new maiden marks the pattern of what she has seen: within, without, not two. Here is the place, here is where everything changes.

It is quiet beside the river. Little birds skim the surface of the water. A standing wave spirals over, never the same water, recurring. I walk with my little girl across the big grey rock.

"David thinks this could be where they used to come," I say, "young girls who were turning into women. He thinks maybe they came here after their first bleeding, to be splashed by the water and to make their picture on the rock."

"Did only girls do it, and women? Maybe some men did too, and boys."

"Look!" I call to the men. "I can see the pattern, here in the water at the edge of the rock."

We stay and look, each one of us absorbed in river and stone. David should be getting back to the Gladstone skeletons, but none of us seems to want to leave. The day lingers.

Finally we put on shoes, gather up the children's scattered clothes, walk up to the car and drive back, talking.

On our return at dusk to Gum Tree Lodge, the children run outside for a last turn on the squeaking iron swing, a last good swing before dark. In the changing dusk their evanescent bodies gleam luminous in the garden, bodies of honey and rain, light hearts flying, voices calling into the night. When I close my eyes, the darkness is patterned with circles and suns and stars and gateways of light, ripples in the water, never the same, repeating and repeating. And still the children's voices laugh and shout in the winter air, bright hair streaming, twin hearts flying on the squeaking swings in the darkening day, as the night gets cold and the coloured fairy lights come on among the trees.

When I was a girl, the passage from the swings and handstands and green lawns of childhood into womanhood was marked by pain and awkwardness. At eleven years old, it really hurt, and the blood was more than I could have imagined. There was a river not far from where we lived, but nobody there to teach the grace of how things change. We had no rites to welcome the flowing of blood and generation. There was no rock, no Water Snake. Instead, I remember only the scratchy plastic pants, the clumsy secret pads and girdles, and the shame of changing for sport in a room full of laughing little girls. And I remember the pain, fainting from the pain.

For me, it was a time of shame and confusion, but the /Xam stories I have read say that a young woman during this crucial period of liminality and transformation is full of power, both creative and destructive. If she looks at you, you might be turned for ever into a tree. Therefore she must be secluded, cared for, and the potency of her changing body turned to ritual intervention. At her touch, springs flow.

Water flows, river flows, water in the desert. The new maiden comes to the source of the river, her magical body flowing with blood and birth, her clear gaze full of power, precious as water. The rock is marked with stars and gateways. The spring is adorned with red. The place is engraved by ice and water and human beings, and the myriad engravings are formed in this place.

HANDAXES

Archaeology is like reading a copy of *War and Peace*, the *only* copy, and tearing off each page as you read it. You can never put things back once you've dug them up.

ANTHONY HUMPHREYS

Although visitors come to the museum to see relics of the past, the artefacts on display are often replicas, and the glass cases peopled with reconstructions. But beyond these exhibits, and the parties of schoolchildren who are here to see them, are corridors to rooms and rooms of other things and people. Here at the back of the building is where they are, the excavated things all placed in order, and the archaeologists and historians who do this work, people who dig and sort and make the stories of the past in storerooms, offices and labs.

David has again interrupted his excavation of the skeletons, this time to show us some handaxes. We pass a room full of antique lace and another where someone is studying the very early use of bone tools. Then he takes us to a place that houses some of the most extraordinary artefacts in the world.

The storeroom is stacked with thousands of brown cardboard boxes, boxes piled in rows like books on library shelves, and each one filled with lithic artefacts from excavations in the region: Nooitgedacht, Pniel, Wonderwerk, Kathu Pan, Kathu Townlands, Canteen Kopje, Burchell's Shelter . . .

When a place becomes a site, the earth is dug and measured, sieved and counted, and each thing small or large that is considered at all significant is labelled and put in a box. This is the discipline of archaeology, in which the knowledge of our past is something made from systems and analysis, a scientific practice that is said to differ quite significantly from the haphazard methods of enthusiastic amateurs. When an environment becomes a source of information in this way, its myriad interrelations are sieved and sorted into a collection of discrete objects. Everything that the excavation has unearthed is then encoded in a library of material things, and these things are organised like texts, catalogued and stacked in rows, numbered and graded.

One box of artefacts is labelled Canteen Kopje. Beside it, propped up against the wall, is one of the tools we saw in a photograph at the site, said to be the heaviest handaxe ever found. It is made of andesite, a pale-brown rock, now flaked by monstrous blows to shape this thing for a use which we can only guess at. Cleaving hippopotamus bones to get at the marrow? Some kind of ritual or display? Were they giants who walked the earth a million years ago and bashed the rocks to make their tools? What powers did they wield? What terrors visited their dreams? The stone is perfectly, inaccessibly silent. I pick it up and it is cold and weathered smooth and really, really heavy. It seems much heavier than the 7.7 kilograms it weighs. I cannot hold it for long. I put it down. Next to the heaviest handaxe is one of the longest hand-axes ever found. Again, I witness its size, 38.5 centimetres in length. Again I hope that actually seeing it here, this real thing, might catalyse some understanding.

The silence of these stones reminds me of a remark made by JM Coetzee in an essay from the 1980s on South African poetry. Pointing out how often our poetry has been concerned with the interiority of things, with silent rocks and stones that do not speak back or answer the speaker's need for a response, he considers why this quest which he calls "so evidently fore-doomed" has persisted for so long. The explanation he suggests is that the continued apprehension of silence could be a mark of failure on the part of the poet, the failure to conceive a peopled landscape, or a society in South Africa in which there is a place for the self.[42]

I think I understand what he means. But there can be another sense in which the silence of stones or other things is powerful precisely because it evokes the irreducible presence of that which eludes the net of human text. When stones, water, fire, wind – the wordlessness of these things and their interrelations – challenge the self's pre-eminence in this way and meet with silence the urgent need to name or tell a story, we can surely be grateful for the teaching.

Although they are cultural artefacts, human tools or even in some sense "texts", the worked-off stones in the museum storeroom are so unimaginably old that they are empty of further explanation. Now, as before, this stone is stone. And now, as usual, the restless narrative mind skids off in search of symbol, metaphor, story, some other exceptional thing.

"Where is the extremely beautiful one," I ask, "the really special one from Kathu Pan? Can we see that too?"

In Cape Town, Duncan told us about a particular handaxe that was dug up at Kathu Pan. He called it beautiful, said it was something like "the defining human artefact", the earliest thing known that is undoubtedly an aesthetic work.

"Yes, here it is," David says easily.

Here on a shelf among the cardboard boxes is this rare thing.

"May I hold it?"

"Yes."

The form is perfect, a perfect almond stone. The fine flaked edge is smooth and even, shaped to a precise point. The handaxe is a tool constructed from banded ironstone whose contour layers of dark and reddish brown resemble the striped fur of an African wildcat, or the grain of an old wooden cupboard, or strands of long hair bleached in the sun, or the ripple of a mountain range across the land. My warm hands touch the 600 000-year-old edge, hold in my very hands the weight of this fine work in which each flaking of the stone has lit the bands of colour into crescent waves, waves of stone wakened by other hands long dead, the touch of their work still warm in this smooth flow of stone. Excavated from the deep loam of the years, the layering of dust and generation, this first beautiful thing rests in my hands now. Seeing, I recall the sunlit flow of rippled rock and water in the river at Driekopseiland. Here it is again.

"Yes, it is the same pattern," Michael says when I show him. "But look, the banded layers of the rock are horizontal. They're strata, flat, layer upon layer. The ripples look like a natural formation, like waves in water. But really they are only there because the rock has been worked, each flake. It's culture, technology, something made. The person who made the handaxe made the pattern."

So here we stand among the assembled boxes, holding this beautiful thing in our hands. The person who made the handaxe made the pattern, a hominid ancestor older than our species who recognised and made this ripple in the rock. Our words are gone and we are silent before it, holding the fine, worked tool in our hands, light breath passing over stone.

Beyond in the storeroom the less exceptional tools are stacked in rows and lines. Their ordered assembly evokes in me a cry for all that is lost and unremembered in this collection, so that here amid the gathering of excavated things I want to grieve what seems like plunder, the powers and disciplines which brought this wealth of conquest from the earth of its particular places to this location, to mourn the unrequitable compulsion of our kind to organise the living world.

Although the discipline of archaeology may be constructed to analyse and know the meaning of the past, the worked stone tools are wordless, irreducibly stony. As humans we seem compelled to understand, but the stones are silent and opaque, empty of story. Perhaps stones, even these ones whose pattern is shaped by human hands, are things beyond the reach of words and texts. They are things that are solid and will not speak or yield to our investigation. As my UWC colleague Tony Humphreys, an archaeo-anthropologist, said to me before we left Cape Town, "Many a career has been trashed on the Early Stone Age. You can spend a lifetime measuring handaxes."

And yet again, as I grasp in a warm hand an arbitrary artefact from one of the boxes, it seems that each stone tool might bear some memory of our original mind. Walking among the organised stacks in the quietness of thousands and thousands of lithic artefacts, I notice how the tender human body seems always washed with feeling, transient tides of wonder, sadness, rage and fear. I notice how the mind seeks out difference and opposition, comparing the wordless stones (the pure thusness of their presence) and the explanatory systems that would seek to understand them, or this warm brief flesh and the profusion of stone tools that endure. I see how the mind loves story and structure. The mind loves pattern.

Perhaps it has always been so. This mind shapes stones to fit the hand, flaking a cutting edge that will reveal the flow. This mind is one that works and makes, fitting and organising the world to our insight and our desire, making things and words and songs and systems, a feeling human being flushed with tides of pain and joy.

In the McGregor Museum collection the tools from Kathu Pan, including the one we think of as the master handaxe, are each labelled with the number 6538 on one side, written in neat black ink. For the last time I touch the smooth old almond stones laid out in their cardboard box. They are red and golden and rippled brown, worked stones that hold the trace of numberless generations of our kind, each artefact assigned a number during the last brief breath of the twentieth century.

In this storeroom the artefacts that recall the shape of human mind are wordless things, tools or weapons or first texts of our culture. Now, through an effect of silica that has glazed the surface of the stone during hundreds of thousands of years underground, the handaxes from Kathu Pan gleam. They are beautiful things and heavy, gleaming.

FLAMINGOS

It is not only that there is water in the world, but there is a world in water. It is not just in water. There is also a world of sentient beings in clouds. There is a world of sentient beings in the air. There is a world of sentient beings in fire. There is a world of sentient beings on earth. There is a world of sentient beings in the phenomenal world. There is a world of sentient beings in a blade of grass.

DŌGEN

What to do next, after what we have seen? We feel peculiar, want something to consume. The museum shop is cluttered with lacy boxes and scented candles, but there are no photographs of hand-axes, no images or replicas of ancient things, not even wildlife posters. Michael and the children want food, groceries from Pick n Pay, a toasted sandwich, tea.

I order rooibos and he has real tea. Sophie and Sky have chocolate milkshakes and share a sandwich. Through the café window we see two people walking past whose features look just like the Bushmen in the tourist books. The old woman is small, her face lined with a thousand wrinkles. Her cheekbones are distinctive, and she has tied a bright cerise scarf about her head. The young woman beside her carries the bags. Her lips are soft, her dark eyes clear and bright. Her skin is smooth as honey. Where do they come from, where are they going? Looking through the glass, I see they see us looking. We nod and greet and turn away.

After tea I feel a determination to buy a poster for the twins of two baby bat-eared foxes that we saw in the museum. We dash to Nature Conservation, but their office has closed. How about finding a piano in a shop for Sky to play? We drive around the city urgently, but the music shop seems to have disappeared.

Then someone remembers the flamingos. This time we take the dirt track off the national road, down to a stinky wet subway under the railway line near the Flamingo Entertainment World. Two ground squirrels stop to watch as we clamber up to the track.

"Look at this, and this!" Michael says, bending to pick up stones. The artefacts are simply lying among the railway gravel. "They were certainly here," he says, "the old guys. We know they liked to hang out near water. I'm sure if you dug here you'd find another site."

Once you can recognise the form of a worked-off edge, the artefacts appear before your eyes again and again. Before that, they are almost invisible. Michael puts a few of the stones in a plastic bag to take to the people at the museum. Maybe they'll come over and have a look, another site perhaps to add to the collection.

The first time we saw the flamingos from the national road, the great population of pink birds outside the city seemed to me like some ancient flowering of tender life which persists in the midst of industrial civilisation. Like a perennial spring in a parched land, this throng of wild birds, chattering and flying. Since then David has told us that the abundance of Kamfersdam exists not in defiance of the city, but ironically because of it. Like the Riet River at Driekopseiland, the wetland used to be more seasonal. Now the pan is being topped up daily with treated sewage effluent and storm-water runoff. It is full all the time, quite smelly, and the birds seem to love it.

According to Mark Anderson, an ornithologist who studies the flamingos, the effect of the artificial pollutants seems so far to have been good for the birds. In recent years the pan has become the most important site for Greater and Lesser Flamingos in South Africa, with a record count of 23 364 in 1998. But the birds have difficulty breeding here, and Mark and others are worried that the hundreds of tons of salts and phosphates and faecal bacteria that flow into the closed system of the pan each year might be turning the water into a nasty soup which could, in time, drive the flamingos away. So they are asking for proper consultation about the future with all the stakeholders – all the human ones, that is.[43]

We stand and look as they feed and fly: on the pan beyond the railway line, uncountable flamingos. One startles, flaps, and soon a thousand long-legged birds are flying. Thousands and thousands stay, chattering on the water.

Like the Kimberley diamonds whose clarity reveals a universe of interpenetration, the colony of flamingos seems to reflect the patterns of a myriad things. Each slender bird is made of pink and paler feathers, a sharp beak, long legs, delicate feet and the sounds of all the others, calling. Each one is fish and mud, wings and eggs, sewage and fertiliser, and the city's quest for lasting treasure. Each beautiful bird is born like this of all the other things and beings, a clear jewel empty as water and full of all the world.

We try to photograph the flamingos, but the chattering crowd is impossible to capture. Pink lotus land blooming in the city's effluent.

ARCHAEOLOGIST

The next day Peter Beaumont is waiting for us at the museum, a tall man with sparkling eyes, wild hair and a friendly smile. Retired now, he is said to have trained under Raymond Dart and has excavated sites all over the region. We gather that in the contested territory of archaeology he is a contentious figure. But if anyone can tell us about Kathu, it will be Peter.

"This is an exciting day," he says. "A farmer out Kuruman way called the museum to say he'd found what looked like a dinosaur skull. You know, ninety-nine per cent of the time, these calls turn out to be a dead end. Natural formations often look like fossils. But he's found three of them, and the pictures he sent look pretty convincing. Look over here."

He shows us the printout of a stony creature with clearly defined eye socket and jaw. "Look at that, funny thing it was." Peter mimes being a dinosaur, forearms raised like claws. "Anyway," he continues, "the museum director and I are going to be at a meeting this afternoon at Wonderwerk Cave, so I've got him to agree to go to the farm and have a look. Are you coming too, Karen?"

Karen van Ryneveld is an archaeologist who works in an office that used to be Peter's. She says, "I'd love to, but I've got a deadline tomorrow."

"Oh well, don't say I didn't try and persuade you."

We walk over to the room where the handaxes are stored. I settle Sophie and Sky on the floor with pastels, paper and yet more chocolate digestives, while Michael gives Peter the package of worked-off stones we found along the railway line.

"I thought you'd be interested. Maybe another site."

He looks at each one, puts them aside.

"Yes, they are flaked all right. But you know, in the Northern Cape, if you can't find a stone tool somewhere within a metre of where you're standing, there's something wrong with you.

"Have you seen these ones?" He indicates the giant handaxes.

"Yes."

Michael points out among the collection from Canteen Kopje a sharp-edged handaxe he found at the site the other day and gave to David in case someone else nicked it.

"Oh, that's virtuous," Peter says, laughing, "too virtuous for me! You've seen this one from Kathu Pan?" he asks, picking up the master handaxe.

"Yes, it's the most beautiful thing, extraordinary."

"You know, some people, Richard Klein, for example, have put forward the idea of what they call the human revolution. Around 50 000 years ago, we became modern. The earliest representational art we know of comes from the Danube Corridor."

"But what about before that? It sounds wrong."

"I think it's rubbish," he says, continuing with emphasis, "I'm a gradualist. You know, forming words, understanding what someone else is saying . . . It seems to me that the capacity for language is something very refined and complex. It must have taken at least a few hundred thousand years to develop. And aside from that, we know that red ochre was used in Africa 400 000 years ago, maybe as early as 800 000. And we found specularite down in the Fauresmith layers." His voice is full of the joy of discovery.

"Specularite? That far down?"

"Yes, specularite. You know, the glittery rock. It's mined at Postmasburg and we found it 200 kilometres away at Canteen Kopje. It was in a red sand layer, along with Fauresmith artefacts that predate 350 000 years ago. They must have been moving it across great distances. So my own view is that the capacity for self-awareness begins with *Homo rhodesiensis*. Nowadays people want a date for everything. So I'd say as early as 1.2 million years ago, maybe 1.3."

In this room the unimaginable years shrink to simple figures. Peter must have told this story of our creation many times before, but it still holds his passion and our attention.

He explains: "I believe this is where it all happened. Southern Africa is the cradle, and here in the Northern Cape the climate was a little kinder and there was higher ground that was fairly free of malaria and other diseases."

"You mean they could live longer?"

"Life expectancy was short. But here, perhaps, they could be a bit healthier, live a little bit longer. It may have given them more time to develop culture and pass it on, here in the Northern Cape."

"Peter, can you tell us about Kathu?"

"Yes," he says a little apologetically, "you must stop me, or I'll just go on and on. Okay, Kathu. The pan site was first reported by a farmer, a nice chap, Viljoen. There was a sinkhole on the farm, and the farm children were playing in it. Then they noticed these handaxes sticking out of the sides. Their father called the museum."

I remember reading that at Kathu Pan, along with a number of fine handaxes, archaeologists dug up a great collection of tooth fragments from the extinct elephant *Elephas reckii*. This helped to date the artefacts they found.

I say, "What about the elephants? I have the idea that they were young."

"Yes, they were mostly youngish. You can tell from the teeth, like these ones." He shows us a fossil tooth. "But we don't know what they were doing there."

"And Kathu Townlands?"

"Well, a while later Iscor was mining an area outside Kathu for road gravel. Someone noticed that there were lots of what looked like flaked stones among the rock they'd dug up. They called the museum, and of course it turned out that they were all artefacts. The place is what became known as Kathu Townlands. When I excavated, we found 9 000 artefacts per cubic metre! That was in the first part. We tried again in another area and again we found 9 000 per cubic metre, and again the same in another."

"How extensive is the site?"

His words are chosen with an old-fashioned care for precision of expression: "I've never had the time to trace it to its end."

"And how many artefacts do you think there might be?"

"We've estimated ten to twenty billion. A friend from North America wants to get a field school going there. Bring out a group of students who can check our estimates, excavate cubic metres across the site, have a look."

"It's unimaginable. What was going on? You think it was a workshop? The banded ironstone that they used comes from Kathu, doesn't it?"

"Yes, it does, and yes, it probably was a sort of workshop. But the site doesn't cover an enormous time period. Maybe ten to twenty thousand years, one or two interglacials."

Here among cardboard boxes that house the traces of our ancestors, here where only stone endures, the stories of people are told as brief warm times between long years of cold. During the last 2.5 million years the pattern of ice ages on Earth is said to have assumed a pulse of about 100 000 years. This means that there are 90 000 years or so of cold, the glacial period, and then there is a warmer patch, an interglacial, for about another 10 000 years. Peter thinks that one or two interglacials are all it took to make the multitude at Kathu. Not long, he says, just maybe 10 000 years, or 20 000, perhaps.

At present, the Earth is approaching the end of another interglacial, the Holocene. It began around 12 000 years ago, along with the first signs of agriculture and settled herds. Following the pulse of previous glacial cycles, global climates should now be starting to get cooler again. But this time, for the first time, the newly civilised Earth is heating up, and it seems possible that the pulse of glaciation and interglacials may be delayed for a while by a global warming of human origin.

Peter continues, "There would have to have been big populations going to Kathu from elsewhere to make the stuff. You don't get this stone in the Kalahari."

We shake our heads and say words like "extraordinary" and "incredible".

I tell him that Kathu Townlands is what got us going on this trip. Duncan Miller had told us about the site, and we wanted to see for ourselves.

"It sounds as though it ought to be a national monument, even a World Heritage Site."

"It's a staggering place," he says. "I've taken various people there, researchers from overseas, and they're awed. You can't fit it into any prevailing notion."

Michael tells him about the two high-quality stone tools we have at home which he inherited from his father, a gift to Jack Cope from Laurens van der Post in the 1970s. Where he got them we do not know, but it was probably somewhere in the Northern Cape. Michael describes how the dark one, a long thin blade, Middle Stone Age, is smoother on one side than on the other.

"It looks sandblasted," he says, "you know, lying face down, I would think, the sand blowing across it and smoothing the upper side."

"Probably wind-blasted during the last ice age," Peter says. "The speeds were higher."

Standing in the storeroom among the assembled tools, cardboard boxes stacked and labelled and stored in rows, plastic bags of stones, dusty hoards of generations dug up in the last brief moments of human habitation, standing here among the silent, ordered things, we twenty-first-century people, digging and talking, I seem for an instant to apprehend those winds, the endlessly cold, cold winds blowing across this land for 90 000 years, the chaff swept off and away. And my heart is full of the fear of that relentlessness, the cold winds blowing across the earth and nowhere to shelter, long winds of the ice age, endlessly blowing.

But here we are now at the museum, and the day is warm. On the other side of the room the children seem to be doing all right among their sprawl of pastels and biscuits, but I doubt that they will be able to last much longer without some attention from us.

"Oh look," I say to them, "there are the skeletons. Remember? We saw them being dug up."

David's bags of bones. Near the doorway of the storeroom, the plastic bags holding the grubby bones of the hundred-year-old dead from the Gladstone site are stacked in labelled piles, two bags per skeleton, more or less. In other rooms lie the uneasy remains of Khoe-San people which the museum acquired in earlier years, bones received in shady circumstances from people who had dug up other people's graves.

Echoes of Sarah Baartman and other curiosities. Skeletons in the cupboard, as they have been called.

"Hmm," Peter says with a shiver, "not for me. I prefer this one. It's from Canteen Kopje, found about three metres down by a diamond digger. We don't know how old it is."

He hands Michael the Canteen Kopje skull, a strangely broad one. We each hold the death's-head in our hands, big old brain, remnant of someone who once lived near here, alive as you or me.

"They were really big guys, weren't they?" Michael says. "Look at the width of the skull from the forehead to the back. It's a massive brain."

"Yes, it's 1 700 cubic centimetres. Brains got bigger and bigger. Then, around 200 000 years ago, they started to get smaller again. Natural selection, I'd say, the constraint of women's hips, giving birth."

Peter is looking at his watch. He says, "You know, I'm going to have to go. We've got that meeting at Wonderwerk Cave, and we have to look at the fossil before that. Would you like to come along, follow our car? You're going out that way anyway today, to Wonderwerk Cave. Don't you want to see the dinosaur?"

I look at Michael and he indicates that I must decide. It is not on my itinerary, but it would be churlish and silly to say no.

"Of course," I say. "We'd love to."

"And you, Karen, are you coming?" he calls to her where she is still working. "Don't you want to have something named after you, maybe a small tortoise?"

He is persuasive and funny, and finally she agrees. All right, she'll come, miss her deadline. For a while we all hang around, have tea with the museum staff at a long table, talk about the dog that Peter and his wife are going to get from the SPCA the next day, and wait for Colin Fortune, the museum director. I see my plans for the day slipping away.

At last everyone is assembled and we set off excitedly. Peter is smiling, ebullient, leading the quest, almost capering.

"*Tyrannosaurus beaumontii*, here we come!" he shouts as they all get into the museum director's 4x4, laughing.

TREASURES

It's a long way to Kuruman, about 200 kilometres. We stop to buy two boxes of Smarties, some bread and milk. All along the way, red-and-white cellphone pawks thread the network of virtual things across the sky, thin voices talking without wires or telephone poles, invisibly connected. After thirty pawks, Sky stops counting.

Watching the wild land speed by, the children, deprived of television at home, pretend that the world viewed through the glass square of window is a TV programme. As the patterns of scrub and tree change to Kalahari sand and veld, a landscape of thorn trees, red earth, grasses and anthills flashes past. Each anthill has been dug out with a dark hole that speaks of a long, delicate nose, strong digging claws, and the pinkish-white body of an aardvark covered in red earth. Sophie and Sky have seen a picture of one in our book of mammals and they think it is adorable. They both want to marry the aardvark.

Driving further and further from the city towards what has been called the heart of the land, we try again to imagine the people whose tools have remained behind. Before leaving Cape Town, Michael searched for *Homo erectus* on the internet, and found a picture of a large, low-browed person with staring eyes, who looks like a cartoon of skin-clad cavemen with clubs and stupid faces, or the cavechild depicted on the wrapping of prehistoric chocolate eggs from Woolworths that someone gave the children to eat on the journey. Since then we have seen the museum dioramas in the Ancestors' Gallery in Kimberley, read various timelines, and held the tools in our hands. But while these reconstructions crowd into our heads like the empty masks of a dream, we still do not know, cannot really conceive of who these ancestors might have been, human beings, here.

Around midday the new 4x4 ahead of us turns off onto a gravel road. Bump, bump, bump – their vehicle is built for this, but our little city car is not. Dust comes through the windows and stones jar the suspension. At last the farm road leads past dogs and thorn trees to a house and a gate.

The farmer, who is tanned, blond and bearded, comes smiling out to greet us, shakes our hands.

"You say it's already been identified?" I hear Peter asking.

"Ja, ons het die ander een Kaapstad toe gestuur."

"Wat het hulle gesê?"

"Nee, dan vloek ek!" Laughing. "They said something about 1952. First discovered then."

Suddenly the treasure quest has lost a little of its joy. While Sophie and Sky dash onto the lawn to play with the farm dogs, the rest of us walk sedately up to the verandah to see the rocks collected on the table. Big quartz crystals, pieces of banded ironstone, and then the skull.

I hold it in my hands, the small dinosaur's skull, its eye socket and jaw, and try to think of it here. Deep, before all people.

"I'll take you to where we found him," the farmer says.

We climb into the back of the 4x4 and drive across the farm. The place where he takes us is a little quarry. Like everyone else in this part of the world, he has been digging up rock. Who knows, maybe he was looking for diamonds. We prod at the piles of banded ironstone and I pick up a piece of crystalline white quartz, the clear shafts marked with red earth and dark lichen.

"Oh, that's a beauty," Peter says warmly.

"May I have it?" I ask the farmer.

"Ja, seker."

He takes us through a fence and under thorn trees to another place where, he says, the ground is white with crystals, white like snow. I ask Peter what he thinks about the dinosaur.

"I don't think it's a fossil," he says quietly. "I've seen too many natural formations that look as though they could be and aren't. Still, it's not my field. We'll wait to see what the Iziko guys have to say."

Sophie picks up a clear quartz crystal and Peter finds one for Sky. The farmer says it's fine for the children to have them. Michael recognises worked-off stones and puts them down again. Little scrapers, Later Stone Age.

As we are about to leave for Wonderwerk Cave, the farmer stops to appeal to Peter: "Sê vir my ek is nie verkeerd nie. Tell me I'm not wrong."

He answers with gentle formality and a bow of the head, "Ek dink . . . it's difficult for me to say this in Afrikaans. I think it's very commendable that you've taken such care with this. I'll follow it up with Cape Town."

Returning to the car, the children's shirts are full of snow-white crystals, treasures for their treasure boxes at home.

Sky says, "The trouble with treasures is that you don't have much time to do things with them."

"Yes," Sophie agrees, "and there isn't even much that you *can* do with them."

WONDERWERK

At the base of a hill near Kuruman, in a place of grasses, is the dark mouth of a cave. The cave is wide and very deep, extending far into the body of the hill. Until the first property owner built a farmhouse on this land, people had been living in the cave since the beginning. The roof is black from their fires, and the floor holds traces of their habitation.

The cave is fenced now and excavated. The fire is out, and the people who come are visitors. Yet the swallows return to their nests each spring, and, climbing the hill, you can see fine, tough plants still growing, and beyond, the blue rim of the world.

Like many other farms whose names evoke the joy of a longed-for homecoming, names like Weltevrede or Welverdient, the property was called Wonderwerk, a miracle. The first white owner, NJ Bosman, lived with his family in the cave from 1900-1907 while the farmhouse was being built. After that they used it for a stock shelter and a wagon house, and for several years in the 1940s mined a layer of prehistoric deposits, which they sold as bat guano for use as fertiliser.

The first archaeological excavations of Wonderwerk Cave began at this time, after someone noticed bones and stone artefacts in the so-called guano. Then, from the late 1970s onwards, Peter Beaumont and others worked on the site. We understand that their findings, as yet largely unpublished, will change some aspects of the way the Stone Age is understood.

Passing through a gated entrance, Michael parks the car near a cluster of small face-brick buildings. Across the mouth of the cave is a big steel railing. I had not expected this here, keys and a gate. But there has been vandalism and graffiti in the past and the barrier is probably necessary. I interrupt the meeting in the little information centre a few metres away to ask for the key. Peter comes out and offers to escort us.

"I really don't mean to take you out of your meeting."

"Oh, there are various reasons why one might want to be out of a meeting," he says. "I can have a smoke, for one thing."

"Well, we're really lucky to have a world authority as our tour guide."

"I don't know about that. I feel a bit chastened after that dinosaur."

The cave is huge. It stretches 139 metres into the hillside, Peter says, and is about 17 metres wide, big enough to keep a fire. A single giant stalagmite stands inside the entrance, like a seated guardian planted at the threshold. There are paintings, what is left of them, on the wall near the mouth of the cave. Painted buck, fingermarks, wriggled lines and stripes seethe ochre and white on the surface of the rock, traces painted over other traces, layer on layer, touch of hands on stone, successive generations.

Peter switches on the halogen lights and the darkness beyond is illuminated. The excavation of the site reaches as far back as you can see. Deep trenches lie on either side of the narrow walkway that leads into the hill, and the entire floor of the cave has been dug and marked up with squares of string that stretch a horizontal net, like a perspective drawing converging to a vanishing point in the distant dark, each square labelled with a small piece of paper, so that, looking back into the cave, the space is hatched across with lit-up string squares that mark the darker regions of excavated earth, their bright labels gleaming in the light.

I give the twins each a small box of juice. The layer of dust on the ground near the entrance of the cave is thick and they want to pound about, stirring it up. Peter looks concerned.

"Don't do that," I say.

Peter tells us that Wonderwerk Cave is the only known place in the world that has been inhabited whenever it was possible from about 1.2 million years ago until the early twentieth century, when the last people who lived here were the Bosman family. The information is so extraordinary that it is difficult to absorb. This cave is home.

Then he starts to show us Excavation 1, a great squared-off hole on the left side of the walkway, fenced with a steel railing.

He begins: "As you go back into the cave, it averages day and night temperatures. It would have been warmer inside during an ice age . . ."

As the informal discourse takes shape, Sophie and Sky, having now finished their juice, disappear along the walkway between the trenches, running away into the gloom together. Peter is talking with enthusiasm about the site, but I am beginning to feel panicky. Just five years old, and they have run far away into the dark, and I can no longer see them.

"I must just see what the children are doing," I say, and leave the conversation.

Back, far back into the dark, big cave, treading along the narrow path between excavated trenches and the deep pits left by the "guano" diggers, walking into the cavernous body of the hill, back, back into the fire-blackened cave, far into the prehistoric dark, I recognise my children. Red corduroy and blue, the modern dyes gleam in the darkness.

"Mommy, come! Hold hands, tight!"

They are standing at the end of the walkway, gazing down into the pit. We look about the cave together and imagine aeons of mothers holding babies in their arms, little ones learning to walk, children play-ing hide-and-seek, mothers giving birth, people sleeping, singing, play-ing, making tools, making music, over and over again. And always there is the fire, the fire-blackened walls.

Together we walk back to where the men are talking, two warm small hands in mine, two small bright bodies, skipping.

"Look," Peter takes up the thread when we return, "you see that lay-er of ash down there? It's the fire ash, one million plus years old. We found thousands of burnt bone fragments with it."

This is the ash from their fires a million years ago. This is the evanes-cent ash. Light flame of life burned hot, here at the hearth where food was cooked and people sang and the fire burned bones and flesh. Danc-ing, singing, healing, the stories of bodies took shape and were con-sumed in the burning of this flame. And this is the ash from their fires.

While other beings make tools and sociable culture, only we have learned to burn. And this here now is ash from the fire that makes us human. This is the beginning of burning. Wood, coal, fossil fuels, combustion. And this is the hearth, the deep, long, buried continuity of our kind, pale ash in the ground, fire ash soft as a pigeon's back, light ash from their fires, this hearth.

"We know that they made grass bedding," Peter continues. "There's a bedding layer at 400 000 BP[44], silica traces from the grass. When you look at the handaxes under a microscope, you can see that some of them were used to cut grass."

He turns to me then, his face lit with delight, "Can you believe that at 200 000 years we found actual grass, quite preserved, like ordinary grass? The cave is extremely dry, there's incredible preservation."

They used stone tools to make grass beds. And here is the womb of the years, which holds the layers of transient grass. Archaeologists like Peter, who dig in the deep loam of habitation, unearth the actual grass layers where they slept, grasses cut with worked stone tools, light grasses growing on the hill. There was love in this place, and sleeping bodies, human people curled together within the sanctuary of the cave. Each stalk collected with the others recalls the imprint of their sleep and the warm crush of their desire, fragrant bodies brief as grasses on the hill.

"It's like a pyramid – it preserves things," Peter says. "We found that porcupines were living here ten thousand years ago at the end of the last ice age. When you crush the droppings, they still smell of porcupine, ten thousand years later.

"There was also a horn core from a sort of blesbok, and bones of *Hipparion*, the three-toed horse from the Middle Pleistocene. It's really dry in here. Really dusty, too. No matter what mask you're wearing, everyone's coughing up black dust after half an hour of excavation."

For Peter, the vertical cross-section of excavated earth is layered as years, stratigraphy read as a map of time. In this cave, he explains, a centimetre equals about a thousand years.

He says, "I brought some gardeners here from the museum one day, wanted them to see where I spent all my time. I showed them the excavation, the layers, and I said to them that in those layers a human lifespan is about one millimetre. One man said, 'You mean my life's only that much?' And I said, yes, that's what it is."

"How did the dust get here?" I ask. "I read somewhere about aeolian sands. What a beautiful name, it reminds me of Coleridge."

"Yes, the wind-borne sands, blown in from the Kalahari. But here it seems to be something different. It's quite sheltered inside."

"Maybe they walked it into the cave," Michael says. "I remember as a child living at Clifton, if we hadn't got all the beach sand off our feet when we came into the house, the floor would soon be covered with the stuff. It was a basic rule. Get the sand off your feet before you come inside."

"I think you could be right," Peter says, "walking it into the cave."

"What do you think it was like for the people who lived here?" Michael wonders. "You've spent nights and days at the site in different temperatures. What do you think?"

"It was tough," he answers simply. "There were no Post Toasties."

"But of course they knew about the land and the plants in ways that we don't," Michael continues. "We would never know how to keep ourselves alive here, but hunting and gathering people would. I remember reading somewhere that during dry years in the Kalahari when the farmers and cattle people went hungry, it was the !Kung San who helped them gather food."

"Yes, you're right," Peter says. "You know, the first time I went up to Border Cave, we were taken there by a young woman from the area. She was really thin, legs like sticks, and carrying a baby. I thought she'd never make it. Well, halfway up, there we all were, really tired and sweating, and she was fine, not a trace of sweat on her face. And I mean, we were fit!"

I ask about the squares of string marking out the excavation.

"It's the grid. When I began excavation here, instead of using the usual metre measures, I kept to the yard-square grid system set up by BD Malan in 1943. I wanted our findings to be strictly comparable."

The grid. It is called the grid. Of course. Dug up by teams of archaeologists and labourers, in less than sixty years the unimaginably ancient cave became a space marked out in squares. Through the activity of this field work, dividing, measuring, sieving, taking notes, the buried accumulations of human and nonhuman culture, sampled from the remnants of deposit left after the "guano" diggers departed, were turned into a collection of things in boxes, objects of study and forgetting on shelves and tables in the storerooms of museums.

As William Blake described it in the story of Urizen, the Eternals formed a line and a plummet to divide the Abyss beneath . . . and called it Science. Perhaps Blake was not concerned with archaeology. Yet his story is one of gates and grids, a locked steel gate and grids of labelled string. It is a story from the threshold of modernity about the construction of systems and the making of knowledge, about discovery, conquest and control, about enlightenment science and early industrialism and the organised religion of the orthodox church. It is a story of the last brief dust of history, a story of pain and loss and the useless quest for some immutable truth.

Now, if no more virgin territories are left, then digging deep into the dust may yet yield precious objects of information or knowledge for discovery. For a million years and more, people and other animals were here, and their fires gave some light and warmth in the unfathomable dark. And now, in the very brief now of the last small layer of dust, the ancient cave is penetrated and hollowed out, its stones and bones and stories sieved and documented, irrecoverably.

And yet, and yet, Peter's voice is full of wonder: "Do you know we found ochre way down? And there were quartz crystals at levels dated to before 200 000 years and chalcedony at older than 350 000. They were pretty things, beautiful, nonfunctional, you see. They collected them from somewhere else and brought them here."

"Maybe from that farm where we were today?"

"Maybe."

Like us, they loved crystals. Like us, they bent towards the earth, collecting precious things. Like us, they looked for treasure to carry home.

"What goes beyond the excavation at the back?" I ask. "Is it the end of the cave?"

"No, there's a final tunnel. It's blocked by a rock fall, but you can crawl in and peep. There are thousands of artefacts around the entrance, Middle Stone Age. Beyond that, we don't know. There's a dolomitic cavern, a huge chamber continuing into the koppie."

"You must really want to get in there and have a look."

"Yes, of course. But there are difficulties with permits."

In all his excavations of the region, Peter has not found significant human remains. But this is the final tunnel, the dolomitic cavern, the last of the place to be discovered. Perhaps this is where they are, at the end of the cave, the undiscovered.

"Come, Mommy, come!" The children are pulling at my shirt. "We want to see the farmer's pants."

We leave the cave and walk to the little face-brick information centre a few metres away. Peter's meeting is over and they are having tea in the midst of a collection of crystals in glass cases, lithic artefacts, and some archaeological and botanical information about the area. People joke about installing him as the local tour guide.

Near the entrance of the tiny museum the gigantic pair of trousers worn by Peter Eduard Bosman is on display. It says that he was 1.98 metres tall and weighed about 200 kilograms. His hundred-year-old pants are made of good quality tweed. I wonder whether he wore these pants during the seven years that he and his wife, Magdalena, and many children lived in the cave. After the family had moved into the farm-house, some of the fourteen children stayed behind, and it is recorded that the last child born in the cave, after maybe a million years of occu-pation, was Bosman's granddaughter, Cornelia, or Girlie, in February 1914.

"Enjoy the rest of your trip to the Northern Cape," says Colin, the museum director, as we say goodbye.

"We really are enjoying it, thank you."

"It's the undiscovered province," he says, smiling.

It's been a long day, but we'll be spending the night in the small face-brick chalet which has been built beyond the ablution block, not far from the mouth of the cave. Neels Lehule, a slender, soft-spoken man who lives at the site and deals with visitors, gives us the key.

"Would you like to see the cave again?" he asks.

"Later, please. We really would like to see it again, but we want to get things sorted out in the chalet first and feed the children, and then perhaps a walk."

Leaving Michael to make a snack for the children, I go for a small walk on my own. I am full of loss and longing, and need the immediate exertion of climbing the hill above the cave, strata of dolomite and growing things.

Climbing the hill which people have always climbed, I reach a place to sit and look.

While the bones of the ancestors have not been discovered, excavation of the cave has shown that Stone Age people cut the local grass to make their beds and burnt the trees as firewood. My notes identify grasses, bushes and healing plants. There is *Themeda triandra*, rooigras, for bedding and feeding animals; *Pellaea calomelanos*, a fern used for boils, for internal pimples of mouth and nose, for asthma, for head and chest colds; *Rhus burchellii*, taaibos, the tough leaves chewed for chest colds, the berries edible; *Grewia flava*, the brandy bush, its red berries used for alcoholic drink; *Cyondon dactylon*, kweekgras, for healing sores and swelling; *Eragrostis lehmanniana*, knietjiesgras, for colic, diarrhoea and typhoid fever. These plants grow here. These plants grow here still. These ancient families of grasses, berries, leaves. Still here.

The old hill rests in quietness, the hill flows slowly in the flow of stone, ripple of rock, ripple of the small fern growing at the edge where a little water has collected in a crack. Breathing in and breathing out, this is the one breath passing from mother to child and on. In the Wonderwerk hill our bones decay to earth, and grow again into trees and radiating grasses, into the small limbs of striped mice and the bright voice of a little bird that is watching me and singing out to tell the others. Gazing, listening, my words are gone into the calling of this voice. The afternoon is warm. The clouds are white. Each leaf grows according to its pattern. This body sweats and breathes.

Then Michael calls my name from near the chalet, and he and the children come up the hill to join me, Sophie with a grubby Maltese poodle, whom she is encouraging to follow them. Together we climb to the top and see the undulating flow of other hills, their tawny backs like the flanks of a great body at rest. Sitting and resting, we sit where others have sat before, each fold of land and rock known and named, each place remembered, and the wide sky reaching out and beyond to touch the slender blue edge of the world.

I sit and look while Michael explores, finds a few stone tools. Sky taps a rock with another stone while his sister plays with pebbles and cradles the Maltese poodle. Then the children come together to my lap, drink some water and have a biscuit. I tell them about the animals that used to live here before guns and wire fences, and about the people, their fires and beds and pretty stones, and how their stories are forgotten and their bones are gone into the body of the place. Sitting together, here where they sat, the world is quiet. Sky's tangled hair is blond as wild grass in the afternoon sun. Sophie's small shoulder leans into my heart, her warm hand resting in mine. Flesh and bone.

Returning, we follow the path down towards the cave, taking turns to carry the dog, who now refuses to walk.

Back at the buildings, Neels knocks at the door.

"You want to see the cave?" he says. "Kom."

I want to see the dark. I ask if he can switch off the lights.

As we walk back, back into the darkness of the cave, it is huge and silent, but not actually as dark as I would have imagined. Even at the furthest end of the tunnel the late afternoon light still penetrates, and each small label on the square string grid gleams clearly. Neels points out a small mud house on the roof near the entrance of the cave. He smiles.

"Swaeltjies," he says, "swallows. They are gone now, but they come back every year. They like this place to have their babies."

"Lift us up! Lift us up!" the children shout. "We want to see."

"Oh! Look at their house," Sophie says. "Look at the tunnel. I wish I could see the little babies."

If it were summer or even early autumn, we could have seen them here. Wave a hand above a swallow's nest, and immediately the small bright yellow beaks are up and open, shrilling for food, while the parent birds fly about, anxiously watching. But now it is winter and the swallows are gone. Each year they leave and they return. Each year brings new babies and the long flying across continents and seasons. And swallows are rain's things, as Dia!kwain explained to Lucy Lloyd. Given to telling cautionary tales, he said that our mothers warn us it is dangerous to harm them, for they come with the rain and the makers of rain.[45]

To me they are small things, swallows, whose comings and goings trace different routes from those of human traffic. They are small, tenacious things, communities of little ones that endure when other beings have disappeared. Like the striped mice in the veld eating grass seeds and living in holes, or mouse bones in owl droppings which archaeologists use to chart temperature change and date human occupation, the little bones chewed and swallowed and dropped into the body of a cave. Here on the hill some of these small ones have remained. Mice and swallows live here still. Owls, too, still here. How many years.

A man approaches us from somewhere beyond the ablution block where he has set up camp for the night. His eyes are blue and his brown face is lined. He wears a knitted cap.

"Good evening," he says graciously. "My name is Anthony – Anthony Simpson."

We smile and introduce ourselves.

"I've come here to play a Bushman instrument," he explains, "my version. It's something I've adapted from the sort of thing they used to play. I'm going to be at the cave this evening to summon up the spirits.

Around dusk, you know, when it's starting to get dark. I'd like to invite your family to come and listen."

While he is speaking to me, the children have begun to get irritable and are trying to hit one another. I thank him and lead them quickly away towards the chalet.

Later, with the first stars brightening and a big, almost full moon rising among clouds in the dusky evening, we meet at the mouth of the cave to listen.

"I've come to summon the spirits," he says again simply. "It's like a Bushman instrument, but I've added my own variations."

The instrument is something he has constructed himself from a big tin and a piano string tightened with a guitar key. Sitting with us now at the mouth of the cave, Anthony begins to play. He plucks one string, one note, one sound, and all the harmonics. Big moon rising, first stars opening, and a thin string is plucked again and again. Grasses, thorn trees, mice, dassies, a single string plucked. Sitting on the ground at the threshold of Wonderwerk Cave, this sound. Ash, dust, grass, stones, fingers, sound. In the changing light of dusk, one sound and all the harmonics.

I remember William Burchell's story of the man who played the gorah for him in a rock shelter not far from here. Having camped in November 1811 at some location in the foreign wilds of Africa which later came to be known as Burchell's Shelter, he describes the Bushmen who lived there as the most destitute of beings, people of deplorable ignorance whose life was the same as that of the wild beasts, their fellow inhabitants of the land. But in the evening, after giving them food and tobacco, Burchell played on his flute as they all sat around the fire. And later one of the men brought his own instrument to play, the one-stringed gorah. Burchell recorded him in a sketch, which shows a thin man seated on a flat piece of rock, elbows on knees, one forefinger in his ear and the other in his nostril, plucking the single string of a slender instrument, light string stretched across a bow.

While Anthony is playing now in the darkening night of moony clouds, a pale form appears, moving silently towards the cave from among the trees. Neels, dressed in perfect white for the evening, has come to join us. Sitting together, we listen to the single string sounding, a few late modern people assembled, children cuddled against Michael and me, warm shawls drawn close against the cold.

The fire is out. Yet here where people sit at the mouth of the cave, the repetition of this sound absorbs the rhythm of our hearts, fingers plucking the single string, one sound calling up the spirits, calling into the night.

Later, over a supper of couscous and vegetable stew in our chalet, Anthony talks about his childhood in Sea Point in the fifties and sixties. He is about Michael's age, probably went to some of the same parties, but where Michael grew up among writers and books, his situation was different.

"I don't read, you see," he tells us. "I didn't go beyond standard seven. I was a rebel when I was younger, so I left school early. All I wanted then was to get out of school. But now I look back and think I must have missed out on some things, cultural things, because of not really reading. I'll have to do it in my next life."

To the sleepy children he says, "You're very lucky that your parents bring you around the country to places like this. I wish I'd had it. One day you'll be grateful to them. One day when you're older you'll appreciate it."

We ask about what he does for a living and he explains that he makes musical instruments and plays them, travels as much as he can. At home in Zimbabwe he lives more and more simply because stuff just isn't available.

"Most of the time there's no petrol, so I use a bicycle when I'm there. I live on my own. My food is really basic, sadza and beans. I cook on a wood fire, no gas. In a way I'm living more and more like a Bushman. It's fine, actually. I don't mind. It's the way I like it."

He enjoys the food we have cooked, but eats less than we do. After the meal he says good night. His smile is open and unencumbered.

In the evening, when the children are asleep, Michael and I sit outside the face-brick chalet and watch the stars and the moon among the clouds, watch two human figures running in the dark and chasing each other among the moonlit bushes from the direction of Neels's house.

Again we try to call to mind some sense of the people who lived here before. This time we try visualising a long wandering line of human beings walking, with each person representing a generation, maybe twenty years each. The line of generations stretches from the present ones all the way back to this cave.

For a small moment I see. Our flesh is made of theirs. Our bones are formed in their pattern. Our breath is their unbroken succession.

Later Michael says, "I felt them. I was lying on my back on the bed and I felt the ancestors. I felt them walking through. They were treading on my heart."

I feel no spirits, but falling into sleep, I sense the ancient and persistent liveliness of the place. In my dreams the swallows come.

We are standing in the cave in the dream, and the labels on the string grid are shining in the gloom. Suddenly a dark shape flashes towards us, flies over our heads, out into the light. First one and then another and another and another. Neels, dressed in perfect white, smiles. Swaeltjies. Come, he says, I'll show you. Stretching up, he waves a hand in front of the nest and two tiny bright yellow mouths gape at us, shrilling for food. Sophie and Sky say lift us up lift us up we want to see, as the small beaks open wide. And in the dream the parent birds return, darting towards the nest and out again into the light, catching insects in the evening air beyond the cave, first stars brightening in the dusk. In the dream I know that soon the gathering swallows will leave for the long flying far away across the continent, swallows flying across seas and generations, and returning to the cave in the spring. In the dream Neels smiles at the children. Swaeltjies. The baby birds are awake in the fire-blackened cave, frail tenacious things, rain's things, shrilling for food.

Next morning, cuddled in our bed, Sky says, "I wish our holiday never ended."

Almost incredibly, we have woken to the sound of rain, rain in early winter at Wonderwerk Cave. It is the gentle kind of rain for which many of the /Xam stories yearn, rain that touches on leaf and soil, the quiet rain soaking into the land, rain walking on rain's legs across the world. Recording the last stories of a group of desert people living temporarily in a Victorian house in Mowbray, the marbled notebooks of the Bleek-Lloyd Collection are full of rain and the longing for rain, stories of rain's things and rainmakers, of rain sorcerers, waters' people, and of rain's medicine people who could call the rain by plucking a bowstring and leading the rain animal across the land.

Now the face-brick chalet is filled with the breath of rain, the beautiful scent of rain, the tender rain that feeds the land. The veld is misty, quiet, and through the white mist and rain of early morning you can see the great steel gate across the entrance to the excavated body of the cave. Above, the hill gleams green and fawn and dark.

When the rain is over, we climb the hill once more. Walking among grasses, thorn trees, tiny ferns and lichens, the air is full of birdsong. Each particular thing is wet and alive.

Here where they came to cut this grass to make their beds, the air is clear and fragrant. Here among the earth and leaves and little animals which are their flesh and bones, here where they climbed in the utter liveliness of the hill, we climb. Sitting on the quiet summit where human beings have always sat and human eyes have seen the wide, wide reach of sky and hill and grassland stretching far away, we breathe the air. The children sit on our laps and we hold them in our arms. Their eyes are new, their warm skin soft and sweet.

In the cave our life is just one millimetre of dust. The years of iron and steel and all of recorded history measure just a little more. Beneath and before, the deep cave floor extends in a long accumulation of human habitation, long before race or history, a million years or more.

We know that for most of the year the veld in this region is far drier than it is now, no rain for months and months. But now this season of drought recalls the grace of growing things, of plants that wait until rain comes, until the seeds can open. Beyond the brief small breath of our particular dust, the hill continues to flow. Months, years, lifetimes, hundreds of years, thousands of years, tens of hundreds of thousands of years, whatever it takes to heal, the tough joy waits to sprout and leaf and flesh and fur again. Swallows calling, returning home.

Coming down from the hill we meet Anthony drinking a cup of coffee outside the neatly equipped old Land Cruiser where he has spent the night, knitted woollen cap on his head. His clothes are hung out to dry on the thorn tree, breakfast mango pip tossed into the veld. He smiles and waves, then places his palms together. A little bow.

Behind him is the dark mouth of the cave. Beyond the steel gate are the grid, the excavation and the place that has not been excavated yet.

They say the human bones have gone without a trace, yet here is ash from their fires. Here is dust carried in from their feet. Here are the grass beds in which they lay. Ash and dust and grass, the fragile transient things remain. Beyond and above, the rocks of the koppie are wet with rain, misty Wonderwerk hill in the early morning. The layers of dolomite gleam dark against the green, layer upon layer, deep before stories. Standing in this place of habitation, our breath makes mist in the cold morning air.

Here, as in every other quest for a story of origins, the scientists, writers, travellers and tourists like ourselves imagine, measure, photograph and describe the shape of that which was the beginning. But the feel of bodies living in a cave, the smell of dust, the stillness before our eyes elude all metaphors. Perhaps one can simply gesture, perhaps a bow.

Everywhere the veld is alive in the fragrance of grasses and the particular lives of swallows and mice, continuity of the small.

SPRING

"Laws of peace, of love, of unity,
Of pity, compassion, forgiveness; . . .
One command, one joy, one desire,
One curse, one weight, one measure,
One King, one God, one Law."

WILLIAM BLAKE

In Kuruman one shop advertises "Tombstones at Factory Prices", while others display plastic flowers and lettered granite slabs in the windows. Perhaps it is because there is so much dying and so much stone in this part of the country that so many businesses sell gravestones, stone on which to fix the memory and the name, to write the story of a life or find some permanent word in which to give it shape, tablets of stone and granite words to hold the names of things into eternity. I am reminded again of William Blake's Urizen, the engraving of an ancient, long-haired, bearded patriarchal God bent over the iron laws and final truths in his stone book, and of how he inscribes the words of his religion into the Book of eternal brass, and goes on to form the implements of its execution.

When Robert Moffat came to the area in 1820 as a representative of the London Missionary Society to teach everlasting life and the Word of God, he realised that he would have no success in converting the Tswana to Christianity unless he could speak their language. In order to do this he spent two months living in remote villages until he could return with enough Sechuana, as he called it, to preach a sermon. Later, as his command of the language – or at least of SeRuti, missionary language – improved, he made schoolbooks, hymns and a translation of the Gospel of St Luke. In 1831 a printing press was brought to the mission, a wonderful machine which produced over a hundred publications, including, in 1857, Moffat's translation of the complete Bible. And so it was that a range of mutable dialects and languages were standardised, names of things were written down, and diverse peoples fixed in place, made into a book.

Now the four of us wander about the Moffat Mission where Robert and his wife, Mary, worked for nearly fifty years in loyal service to God and to the Africans, whom they loved. In one account, a story of Moffat of Kuruman written for use in Africa, we are told that he had been a gardener in England when he was a young man, and that later he found the patience he had learnt from gardening was needed in his work among the people of Bechuanaland, for he kept on sowing and planting the great thoughts of God and had to wait many years before he saw the harvest.[46] Ploughs, spades, saws, a blacksmith's forge, these new tools dug the land and built the houses, and in time a great stone church, seating eight hundred people, was erected. For Christians, imperialists and others, Kuruman became the crucial node of civilisation on the road to the north.

The single element that enabled Moffat to enact his belief and determination in this way was water. The mission station was built about eight miles from the legendary Kuruman Fountain, or Eye, a natural spring which still yields eighteen million litres of water every day. It is not recorded whether the beautiful water of the Kuruman Eye may in some sense have evoked for the missionaries that water of everlasting life which they had undertaken to share with the heathen, or how exactly they established control of what must always have been a treasured watering hole for local people. But in 1820 Mary Moffat described in these words the spring which marked the end of their journey to the interior:

> The last outspan place was the source of the Kuruman River. It is a vast rock . . . and at every side the most beautiful water that I ever saw . . . gushing out.[47]

Aside from this, we do know that the Eye was to her husband Robert a valuable resource to be channelled into the service of agriculture, and that furrows were dug which led a constant flow to irrigate the station. Like the old churches in Europe built at the site of springs and magic wells and other sacred places, the Word of God in this part of Africa was established at an oasis in the Kalahari, a location which subsequently came to be known by some as the Fountain of Christendom. The marks of its benevolent teaching were a book, a Bible, a school, a church, a road, iron and steel, tools and a printing press, straight furrows and a garden of fruits. By the time the town of Kuruman was formally laid out, the Moffat Mission had ownership of the riparian rights over the spring.

These days the mission station is quiet: a thoughtfully constructed world of stone and thatch and polished wood, water flowing in the furrows and the green shade made of dappled words and prayers. Yet this quietness of refuge and retreat is not the quality of peace originally intended by its founders. There was a time before Bantu Education and the Group Areas Act when the church was full of singing worship, and noisy children played and learned their lessons in the classrooms. Then, when the Nationalist Government closed the school and sent the worshippers back to the areas they were said to have come from, the settlement became uncomfortably quiet. In recent years, people have begun to try and reinhabit the mission, use it for workshops and visitors. But while the water still flows through the garden, I understand that the fruits in the orchard are tiny now.

After walking about the empty buildings, we get back into the car to trace the furrowed stream to its source. Although several signboards direct us to Die Oog or The Eye, the green heart of this Kalahari town (a venue for picnics, photographs and outings) has recently been officially returned to its Tswana name, Gasegonyana, the Little Calabash. The name refers to the cave from which the water flows, a little calabash that never stops pouring. It is an evocative metaphor in a dry land, yet in a sense (as Nancy Jacobs points out in her book *Environment, Power, and Injustice*) that which it evokes no longer exists. For in the 1970s modernist planners remodelled the Eye in the name of efficiency and public good. The cave was closed up, in order, they said, to protect it from vandals, and water siphoned off to supply the town.[48]

This reconstruction was perhaps the most conclusive event in a long story of cultural imposition. After the missionaries' introduction of Western culture to the region, Kuruman was subjected during the twentieth century to a programme promoting the dominance in every field of what the Broederbond described as "uitsluitlik Afrikanerbelange". When the first Nederduits Gereformeerde Kerk minister settled at Kuruman in 1912, he sometimes convened services under the trees at Die Oog.

Then, in 1938, as part of the centenary celebrations of the Great Trek, a monument was erected at the spring with a text sealed up inside it, Professor Gawie Cillié gave a speech about "God en godsdiens en Voortrekkers", and a great festival, "die grootste kultuurfees in Kuruman se geskiedenis", was attended by 4 500 people.[49] In an enthusiastic replay of their ancestors' occupation of the land a hundred years previously, men put on old-fashioned clothes and practised volkspele, while thousands of women wore kappies and long dresses and walked through a dry landscape of stones and a few scrubby bushes to meet the Johanna van der Merwe ox-wagon, which was waiting outside the town.

For the 150-year commemoration in 1988, another plaque was unveiled at the 1938 monument and an event was staged by the Afrikaner

Volkswag, attended by Eugène Terre'Blanche and a large number of other men, riding horses and carrying flags.

A history of Kuruman during this period notes that cultural activities for the English included Boy Scouts and Freemasonry. What the other people were doing is not recorded. As the local historian, PHR Snyman, puts it, "Min is bekend oor die georganiseerde kulturele bedrywighede van Kuruman se swartes en kleurlinge."[50]

Now in the New South Africa, across the road from Die Oog a small brick building announces in sky-blue paint on the window: "Universal Church of the Kingdom of God". A white dove flies against the background of a heart painted in signal red. As we approach the fenced green shade of the spring, the Saturday-morning air is filled with the cheerful sound of "The Girl from Ipanema", tall and tanned and young and lovely, accompanied by the voices of another festival. In the dappled green light on the grass just outside the green iron gate there is a little gathering of stalls selling home-made clothes and pottery mugs, crocheted dogs and fudge, in celebration of something that seems, outwardly at least, to have replaced the kappies and volkspele of earlier years. About thirty people, all of them white, are queueing up to have their hair shaved to a number-two or -three cut and then painted green. They are smiling and photographing one another. One elderly, balding, originally white-haired man now sports a bright green tonsure and bright green moustache. He is braaiing boerewors and laughing. Others walk about, talking excitedly, their short haircuts and the green dye having combined to produce an atmosphere of elation.

Through the garden gate, down the steps, the children run quickly to the fern-filled source, where water falls over rocks and down into a pool of fish. This must be the place where the calabash was sealed and a little water left to be pumped up over the ledge for aesthetic effect. A granite plaque cemented to the rock reads: *Hierdie gedenksteen is onthul deur sy edele B.J. Vorster, L.V., eerste minister van die Republiek van Suid-Afrika, tydens sy besoek aan Kuruman op 4 September 1971.* Beyond, the pool runs into a lake edged with green kikuyu grass and planted with palms and willow trees and other so-called aliens. A tall jet of water fountains high off the surface.

Little is known about the history of this abundant spring and its people and animals and birds before the arrival of the missionaries. But a great water snake did live here, as in all watercourses, and it is known that the cave was filled with hundreds of stalactites and stalagmites. Mary Moffat writes: "I went into the principal cave . . . and went nearly knee-deep in water clear as crystal. The top of the cave is lined with bats, and in some directions we heard waters rushing like a torrent."[51]

Reading these words now, I imagine other women, their voices laughing and calling, unnumbered generations of women, standing and splashing near the torrent where she stood, the missionary's wife, her legs in the water of the source, all splashing, wet.

Besides her account, there are at least two photographs of the Little Calabash from the time just before the establishment of the town in 1890. Zooming the black-and-white images larger and larger on my computer screen, I try to understand how it was then, an utterly different environment. No tall trees, no big pool, no green lawn, no people. It looks like the area around Wonderwerk Cave, an ecology of rocks and numberless grasses, yet I have been unable to find out for certain what particular plants would have grown here before colonial vegetation and modern apartheid planning claimed the spring and turned it into a green dream of Eden. Most likely, here, as elsewhere in the region, the veld was made of vaalbos, rosyntjiebos, swarthaak and so on: medicines, foods, bedding, thatch, and the myriad things that grow outside of human use.

These days the Kuruman spring would probably be unrecognisable either to Mary Moffat or to those people and other animals who came to this source for uncountable years before the changes of recent history. But there is at least one inhabitant whose population seems to have been largely unaffected by human narratives, although it has had to share the place with recent immigrants. A particular species of fish, *Pseudocrenilabrus philander*, the southern mouthbrooder, occurs only here and in other geographically separated islands of water in Southern Africa, in springs and sink holes and coastal lakes. Many of these fish populations have probably been isolated for at least sixteen thousand years. How they came here is not fully understood, but we do know that the isolation over all that time has meant that each body of water has become the home of a distinct version of the species whose colouration and other features have evolved to make it different from all the others.

While the background colour of the southern mouthbrooders at Wondergat is described as grey-gold and their scales are edged with blue, the fish at Molopo Oog are silver-blue, and the ones at Lake Guinas are metallic gold with a green-blue tinge on the flank. At Kuruman Eye the background colour of the fish is called khaki. Otherwise (and here the particularising language of the ichthyological paper begins to take off into something irresistibly beautiful, even psychedelic), males have silvery cheeks with a pink lilac sheen, the lower lip marked with a fluorescent light blue stripe that extends along the lower cheek as a sky-blue stripe. The inner ring of the eye is pale gold, and the iris black, the dorsal flank and dorsal caudal peduncle silvery pink with a blue sheen, the ventral flank and ventral caudal peduncle yellow-gold. The chest and belly are silver-white, the dorsal fin transparent, with blue and magenta checks, and the dorsal fin stripe is black along the whole length of the fin. Pectoral fins are yellow, the pelvics black, fading to transparent grey and white. The anal fin has blue and magenta checks, with a bright carrot-orange trailing edge, and the caudal fin has pale blue and magenta checks, with a yellow tinge on the ventral part of the fin. Females at Kuruman Eye are similar to this, but some of the colouration is paler, and the anal fin is transparent, with blue and magenta checks and yellow anteriorly.[52]

This gorgeous terminology describes the colours of speciation taking place over thousands of years. This is evolution, Darwin's story, a different view of water, fish and life from that which Moffat's books and Bibles carried into Africa. The spring may be the very spot where God's green Garden was cultivated afresh to save us from our parents' sin, yet here are prehistoric fish that swim and breed and change, like an image of continuity and of impermanence.

At the edge of the Eye a father and his small daughter are leaning over the wooden bridge, dropping pieces of white bread into the water. The big orange koi jostle at the surface with whiskered barbels and a great khaki flock – I know the word for fish is "school", but these remind me of a slow flock of birds – a flock, then, of what must be the endemic mouthbrooders. They look much less colourful than their formal description suggests, but the water is so clear that every flick of fin or tail is visible, and each scrap of bread, disintegrating as it sinks.

Beyond this bridge the surface of the artificial lake is almost overgrown with water lilies, recalling to me Monet's installation at the Musée de l'Orangerie in Paris: three oval rooms whose walls are filled with

huge paintings of *Les Nymphéas* and the ceilings made of misted glass, so that the transient clouds and skies over the city pour ever-changing light and shadow into painted lakes of flowers, leaves and water, willow trees reflected in the flow. I believe that near the end of his life Monet gave the set of paintings as "a gift of peace for the nation" after the First World War, and directed that they were to be unveiled only after his death. Now Michael and I remember the wonder of seeing them for the first time, and then of sitting for several hours in the midst of all that shifting light and colour and watching other people entering the room and seeing the water lilies: again and again, the expression of sweet relief on their faces, of rest.

At the Eye the lily pads float the same soft sheen of green silk satin across the water, and the flowers rise from mud into the light. Soft buds, open lotuses, pink and gold. The water is the clearest I have ever seen: clear water all the way to the bottom, a fish swims like a fish. Call it peace or everlasting life, in the clarity of this spring the limpid mind of water and fish and flowers is unobstructed. Sitting on the grass, watching the fish swim as they swim, the ancient ones and the bright red koi, fish swim in water clear in the pink and golden lotus land. Gift of clarity, calabash of water in the desert.

The water at Kuruman changes everything. The spring is an oasis, a sacred site. The water is clear and free. Citizens of the town do not have to pay for it. And yet, as Nancy Jacobs reminds her readers, as soon as it flows beneath the high iron fence surrounding the park, the water enters a landscape inscribed with the delusions of race and segregation.

First it irrigates garden plots that are still predominantly owned by white families, and then, downstream from the mission, the abundant flow shrinks to a narrow ditch that passes through the areas where black people live, ending in the dry river beds of the Kalahari.[53]

On the big road out of town, a trace of that early highway by which Moffat's station of God's Word was linked into routes across Africa and the world for travellers like Doctor Livingstone and all the others, Sophie and Sky notice a big "No Hitchhiking" sign, a crossed-out hiking thumb. They love reading the signs of crossed-out things – no smoking, no fishing, no picking flowers – but they have never seen this one before. I imagine it is something to do with HIV, truckers particularly, and the women who wait for them on the side of the road. I believe that when recently a Quaker man called Richard Aitken was director of the Moffat Mission, there was a project to make cheap chipboard coffins with rope handles. But the funeral industry makes some people in the region really rich, and the project did not get far. The infection rate in the Kuruman district is said to be very high.

Leaving the town, we share a bottle of spring water in the car. Tasting this living source, I wonder about the ambiguities of purity and contact, and the quest for beginnings, for that which goes beyond and before these narratives of pain and loss, for that which may endure. I would like to think that opening up the cave again might help somehow to free the uncontaminated joy of our inheritance, letting the water run, the torrent flow, seeding the garden with local plants, and breaking down the fences. But here at Kuruman the grid of recent history seems, at least at present, to inhibit the possibility of this remembering, or of women splashing in the stream.

Now, at this first node of contact with the great arterial roads to the north, there is so much dying, and tombstones are expensive, more than most families can afford. Here and nowhere else, water is free and clear, water flows continually. The prehistoric fish still swim and eat and breed and change. Out of the mud the pink and golden buds of water lilies rise to the surface and open in the light. But the sacred source is furrowed into segregated yards, and built around with tablets of stone, and while the graves may have been inscribed with the comfort of everlastingness, the fleeting multitudes still pass away, gone without a trace.

BODIES

We have found accommodation outside Kuruman for two nights, a base from which to visit Kathu. An added attraction is that it is a game lodge. I want to see wild animals as well as archaeological sites, and not just microfauna.

After looking at some ducks and crows in cages near Reception, we unpack the car again – luggage, camera, books, soft animals and bags of food – and dump them all inside the chalet. The place is equipped with air conditioning, wildlife posters, fridge and shower, as well as good beds and towels.

The afternoon is late. The sun is low. Sophie and Sky have been whining in the car for the past hour, but now at last we can all slow down and breathe. Thorn trees, grasses, scrub and sand, here among hills the world is wide.

"This would be a good place for doing meditation," Sky says, looking about outside.

"Yes, it would. It's wonderful."

Already Michael is picking up stones beside the road. "Look, a scraper! And here's a cleaver. It's our guys again, Earlier Stone Age."

After a while he says, "You know, Kathu almost seems irrelevant now. This is the place. They're everywhere."

I walk up above the chalets to sit and watch the changing dusk. Everywhere in the red sand of the hill are flaked stones and cores, and the fresh droppings of many creatures. A whitened snakeskin curls against a rock. In the midst of chalets, cars and lightning conductors, sitting here where they sat a million years ago, we breathe the air of hills they may have known as the sun was setting and the day grew cold, here among snakes and other animals, in the delicate changing light of dusk.

Sky comes to join me.

"Look at the beautiful light," I say, "all pink and blue."

"Yes. I like all the wildness. It would be a good place for doing meditation," he says again.

Sophie holds a stone tool in her hand. "Is this one, Daddy?"

"Yes, it is.

"Hold it in your hand," Michael says, bringing a curved, worked piece of banded ironstone to me. "What do you think it was for?"

"Cutting? I don't know."

"Look, it's a scythe, like this." He shows me the action. "It's the only way you can hold it. You know what it's for? For cutting grass."

He finds two unworked stones and flakes off an edge. "Look, this is what you do."

He grasps a handful of veld grass and cuts it off with the stone. "You'd go out into the veld and cut some grass. For a nest, a bed. When you've got enough grass, you just chuck away the stone. Make another tool next time. Gilette disposables."

On the way back to our chalet we meet a group of young men and women dressed in bright colours, laughing and talking as they go.

Michael says, "I'm going to show them what we've found. I want them to see what's here."

He stops the group and shows them the tools he has picked up, passing on what he knows. "You see, it's important," he says urgently. "These tools were made by our ancestors, our common ancestors. Your ancestors and mine. They are the same, for all people. If you go back far enough, we're all South Africans."

One man in particular, bearded and a little older than the others, listens attentively. After a while he nods and smiles. "Thank you. I understand."

A couple of people with American accents come to join the group. They have been to Wonderwerk Cave, they say. They didn't really get the details, but thought it was nice. Michael shows them the tools as well, tells the same story. They seem interested, but do not share our obsession.

"What are you all here for?" I ask as they pass by together, walking down the hill to supper.

"We're educators," a young woman answers. "We've been having a training workshop, HIV/Aids. This is our last night. We're going home tomorrow."

I think of the people we know in Cape Town who are involved in such work, and of the tender body of this struggle which is so full of dying and the relentlessness of love.

"Enjoy the evening."

Later, when the stars are out, we can hear them partying: "In the jungle, the mighty jungle / The lion sleeps tonight", and Ladysmith Black Mambazo singing harmonies. For hours the rhythms beat out into the dark, awakening the valley to dancing and singing, thread of breath and exuberance, joy of human bodies dancing.

Early next morning, the children and I drive around the property, looking for animals. Eventually we see four impalas. We watch them watching us, and then calmly wandering away. Impalas may be the most ordinary of buck, but we are excited. To see a wild being moving freely and at home in the world is always wonderful, even if the story of it must contract in the telling into a list of names, stuffed trophies of our adventure.

After breakfast we have promised to visit the baboons. According to the brochure, the game lodge has a few rehabilitated chacma baboons living with some vervet monkeys. In each case, the baboons have been rescued from horrible circumstances and cared for, sometimes hand-reared. Now the baboons are constrained by a wire fence and a current of electricity that runs along the top, a threshold which the monkeys are somehow able to transgress.

Sophie and Sky like baboons because they are animals. Michael is probably more interested in stone artefacts than caged baboons, but I do want to see them, partly because they are primates. Unlike apes or human beings, the so-called Old World Monkeys like baboons and vervets (whose genetic lineage diverged from ours about thirty million years ago), have tails and walk on four feet, and their social organisation tends to be fairly rigid. Still, they are family – at least in some distant sense.

At the edge of the enclosure, which is about an acre in size, a mother baboon sits holding her baby to her body. As we arrive she looks at each of us intently with very narrowly spaced eyes, then moves nearer to the fence.

"Look!" Sophie says. "The baby is having milk!"

The little baby is drinking from his mother's breast, and the human children are fascinated. They remember with some nostalgia being breastfed together, one on each side. So they recognise the pleasure of this tiny being with pixie ears, his pale face serious as he clings to her fur and moves from one nipple to the other. When he has had enough, his mother rolls luxuriously on her back, legs and arms in the air, while her baby climbs over her body. He wees on her, but she doesn't mind. As soon as he moves just out of her peripheral vision, she turns and grabs him, or moves to watch what he is doing.

Remembering Jane Goodall's description of how she learnt about mothering her own child from a certain female chimpanzee, I imagine that this baboon mother is teaching me too, showing me something that I watch with a sort of yearning. While Sophie and Sky identify with the baby, it is the mother, timelessly being here now with her child, whom I love. Even though she is caged and I am not, and even though I have numerous other supposed advantages over her, I long for a gentleness that is free of the separations and deadlines that life with my own children has always involved, even when they were babies. In the big wire enclosure the mother baboon walks or lolls or plays all day with her child, either keeping him in physical touch, or holding him in sight and within arm's reach. And all day the baby plays and rolls over and around his mother's body. When a little vervet monkey comes to visit, they tumble together for a moment, but soon the baby is back with his mother. When the mother wants to move away, she picks him up with one arm and walks off, or gets him to cling on underneath.

If the baboons were free, she would certainly have to forage, but otherwise I understand that her relation with the young child would be very much the same as it is here. Baboons lactate for about a year, the mothering instinct is said to be extremely strong and the baby is very dependent on the mother. There is also the possibility of infanticide, usually from a male coming in from another troop. So always they are together, touching and watching.

While we are watching them, a bakkie pulls up beside the enclosure. It is one of the owners of the game lodge, who has come to say hello to the baboons. She speaks to them in strange guttural sounds, and they speak back. I ask her about the two older babies who are playing together on a tree, and she explains that they are twins.

"Their mother died, and someone brought them when they were

tiny. People know by now to bring baboons to me when they need to be cared for. So I looked after them for two months, fed them milk and ProNutro. About a week ago I brought them here. Now I just want to see that they're happy."

Scampering on trees, tumbling in the grass and coming up to the fence to greet their foster mother, the little twins are almost always touching each other, and almost all the time the bigger one keeps a firm arm around her smaller sister. My human twins watch closely, fascinated.

"I hand-reared the other female as well," the woman says. "Her name's Jane."

From the point of view of so-called hard science, researchers like Goodall and other primatologists, many of them women, have sometimes been criticised for giving personal names to the objects of their research. Wild animals are neither people nor pets, it is said, and it is misleading to respond to them like human beings. Yet for many people who have lived in close proximity to communities of non-human beings and studied their behaviour, the categories of human and animal being, of researcher and researched, tend to become less distinct in the field than they might appear in the laboratory.

So the primatologist Barbara Smuts has described how studying a troop of baboons in Kenya changed her understanding both of who they were and of her own project. She writes that her movements became those of what she calls a humble disciple, learning from the masters about being an African anthropoid.

Right from the start, she says, the baboons stubbornly resisted her feeble but sincere attempts to convince them that she was nothing more than a detached observer, a neutral object they could ignore. They knew better and insisted that she was, like them, a social subject vulnerable to the demands and rewards of relationship.[54] Smuts goes on to remark that in time she came to know each of the 140 members of the troop as a highly distinct individual. Each had a recognisable gait, a characteristic face and voice, favourite foods, favourite friends and favourite bad habits.

For Smuts the experience of living with these and other animals has led her to see the possibility of relating to nonhuman beings as persons. But instead of personhood being an essential attribute which we may "discover" or "fail to find" in other animals, she believes that it has to do with the quality of our relationship with them. If they relate to us as individuals and we relate to them as individuals, it is possible for us to have a *personal* relationship. If either party fails to take into account the other's social subjectivity, such a relationship is precluded.[55]

In the Bleek-Lloyd notebooks numerous stories document just such relations with animals. Baboons in particular are described as being persons very much like ourselves. And as the only other large primates known to the San, baboons in these narratives often seem to come uncomfortably close. It seems that their culture is not so different from that of humans, and their language and society tend to be experienced as an unsettling presence in the neighbourhood, which needs careful negotiation.

Dia!kwain described to Lucy Lloyd the sentience of baboons in terms of a capacity for language and society:

> My father was the person who told me that baboons speak Bushman. My grandfather also said that they speak Bushman, he told me that. They speak Bushman, speak sounding like Bushmen. When we hear them talking here, we often think that other people are talking . . . when we catch sight of them, then we see that they are baboons talking there sounding like people. Baboons are not like other things, for they have wives they also are like Bushmen. Grandfather said that a baboon puts a stick of s'ó|õä in its mouth, in the cheek. This little stick tells it about things which it does not know. Therefore it seems as if it knew them well, because the stick of s'ó|õä has talked to it about them. Therefore it knows them.[56]

He explained that baboons should not be spoken with, even though when a baboon catches sight of a person he may call our name. Inevitably, for these are after all stories of prohibition, people transgress this rule.

So Dia!kwain tells about a man who was returning with some flour from the white people. When the baboons saw him, he remarked rashly, as the translation puts it, upon their foreheads' steepness. This angered the baboons and they all came down the hill to get him.

"The baboons became angry with him," Dia!kwain says, "because he found fault with them. He said that their foreheads resembled over-hanging cliffs. And they broke off sticks on account of it."

At last the man pretended to be talking to white men and called to them for help. Hearing this, the baboons ran away, frightened.[57]

Often when the taboo against personal relationships with baboons is ignored, the story of this transgression becomes a cautionary tale. /Han≠kass'o tells Lucy Lloyd about the girl of the Early Race of People who married a baboon:

> Two girls were playing. One has some //hara [specularite] and wants to draw gemsbok with it. The other has ttò [ochre] and wants to draw a springbok. Then she says it is //hara, so I think I will draw a baboon with it. The baboon then sneezed because she spoke his name. He decides to change her face into a ba-boon's face. This he does, in time, and in time this foolish girl follows him up into the mountains to be his wife.[58]

Stories like these describe what seems to be an uneasy sense of the compelling personhood of fellow beings who, as potentially aggres-sive primates, occupy a similar foraging niche.

Drawing from a different net of stories, Barbara Smuts gave names to the baboons she was studying – Dido, Lysistrata, Cicero, Leda – that recall with an ironic turn the cultural icons from her own lexicon. Here, as perhaps for all of us, the quality of personhood recognised in other animals holds up a mirror to one's own preoccupations. Like the tales of hominid ancestry at the McGregor Museum, these stories we tell about animals, and especially about other primates, are always in some sense stories about ourselves.

And yet, while we are speaking about the baboon called Jane, she stops what she is doing to come and sit close against the fence and gaze at the woman who reared her. There is more to human/animal relations than the one-way human perspective.

"Jane is really loving to me," she says. "But if I come to visit with my husband, she can get quite jealous and aggressive."

We ask about the other female, the mother holding her baby.

"He was born in captivity, her first child. His father died trying to escape. The electric fence got him."

Michael looks horrified: "He must have been so desperate to be free that he endured shock after shock."

"Yes."

After more friendly communication with the baboons, their foster mother leaves. Jane then turns her attention to looking at us until, having seen enough, she resumes grooming. Whenever she wants to groom someone she announces her intention by grunting repeatedly and chattering her teeth and lips together, up and down, very fast. Then she finds a suitable recipient, usually a particular female vervet monkey. Each time the procedure involves holding the monkey firmly, hugging it close with one arm, then picking through the fur on head, arms and body, while sucking the skin and sorting between the hairs.

"Lice check day," say the twins, whose hair is checked every Wednesday at school.

To me it looks as though she needs someone to mother. She has never had a child and there is no large troop of baboon friends to groom. So the little vervet becomes her baby, or at least her companion. Whatever the monkey thinks is going on, she is very compliant, even pleased. She relaxes completely in the baboon's arms, closes her eyes, and stretches out a limb luxuriously.

While we find all this interprimate co-operation absorbing, Jane is also quite interested in the human beings. She does all her grooming close to the fence and stops every so often to give each of us a long hard look. Clearly, whatever projections we bring to this encounter, the baboon called Jane, our extremely distant relation, has a point of view that is as real as ours. While we are watching her, she is also observing our behaviour.

In the late afternoon the four of us walk up to a ridge of banded iron-stone above the valley. From this height you can see all the way west to a rim of blue hills and Kathu in the distance. In the other direction is Wonderwerk Cave, part of the same extended neighbourhood for people who travelled on foot. I have a camera, but photographs will merely show a repetitive expanse of grey-greenish bushes, not the place itself, beyond and before photographs: scratchy, dusty, stony, and utterly lively, a particular place, known and inhabited.

A few gemsbok appear in a clearing far below. As they turn, for an instant I can see the running flanks of painted buck on a rock wall. Then a herd of springbok pass in the valley, leaping high, like a small memory of the great migrations. While the scrap of wilderness in the game farm is certainly fenced and monitored, the pale wild grass gleams in the afternoon sunlight. The scent of this grass is something transient and particular, the beautiful grass, back-lit in the sun. Here, as before, the world is alive. The world is watching. In the grasses, the tiny life continues in the ancient forms of beetles, ants, butterflies, mice and all the infinitesimal ones invisible to our eyes.

The human family wanders among the stones and grasses on the hill or stops to sit and play. The day is quiet. Barefoot now beside me, her sweaty shoes and T-shirt cast aside, Sophie sits in an easy squat, bent over and drawing patterns in the sand with a piece of stone. The low sun lights up her unbrushed long red hair, red as the red earth where she sits drawing, rapt in this making, as the shadows form in the patterned sand, long hair falling across her face, the soft skin of her arms and back luminous and pale, creamy corduroy pants all grubby from the dust.

At dusk it will be full moon and I want to watch it rising, see the world change colour. We find a suitable big rock to sit on. But Sky is soon restless and Sophie becomes contrary and cross, both of them resisting me now and my numinous desires. I could stay here for a long time, just sitting. But the twins are tired and want to be with me, on me, sitting on my lap, pulling me out of stillness and into their arms. I feel irritable. And then, oh let it be, let it go, remember the mother baboon and how quickly children grow up. Holding a flaked edge of stone that someone long ago left lying on the hill, I cut a handful of grass to show them.

As we wait for the moon I tell them about the Tibetan idea that everything is magnified five hundred times at the time of the full moon, and that it is said to be an auspicious opportunity for ceremonies and meditations. I tell them some of the /Xam names for the heavenly bodies recorded by Bleek and Lloyd. Orion's Belt is three she-tortoises hanging on a stick. The pointers to the Southern Cross are two male lions. Venus is the Day-Break's Great Star. The Milky Way is a handful of ashes cast into the sky by a Bushman girl who wanted light so that people could return home. The moon is one of /Kaggen's veldskoens.

Sophie asks, "When the Bushmen were here was the world all wild?"

"Yes, in the beginning."

"*Really?*" She knows it is so, but seems to want to provoke us.

We try to give them some sense of how things seem to have been for a very, very long time, and of how recently the world changed. Cars roar past on the road to Kuruman and I wonder how they might have sounded to the people who were here before.

"It would have seemed like the end of the world," Michael says. And then, "Well, I suppose it was for them the end of the world."

Out here in the hills the civilisation we carry with us seems both oversensitive and insensitive, a culture so indifferent to place that it can erect a clutter of face-brick buildings right outside the cave at Wonderwerk or seal up the source of water at the Kuruman Eye. Sitting on this rock in the beautiful dusk, how rarefied we seem. How civilised. How vulnerable without our things and our equipment, hapless but well-meaning and passing it all on to our young.

Unsurprisingly the children's disagreeableness reaches a level of mutual provocation which means that they are beginning to hit each other. Quietly, just in time, the first gleaming rim of the full moon appears on the horizon.

"Look!" I say, grabbing both twins and making them sit still on my lap. "This is a special moment. Now look."

On returning to the lodge we meet the owner, and Michael shows him some of the Earlier Stone Age artefacts we have picked up. He looks at them dubiously.

"I think you've got a better imagination than me," he says.

Michael explains how old they probably are, and says how valuable this piece of land could be for educating people about the deep past. We even suggest the benefits for tourism in the region, extending the attractions of the lodge. But the farmer does not share our fascination.

"You can take away as much stones as you like," he says generously. "The more stones you take, the better for us. I've got so much stone."

In the evening when the children are asleep, Michael and I walk outside into the night. The moon is high in a wide sweep of banded clouds, and the darkness is thick with stars. When Dia!kwain told Lucy Lloyd that the stars are things which resemble the moon, he explained that they used in the past to be a person.[59]

In //Kabbo's long narrative of Jupiter, the Day-Heart Star, the star speaks to his child (Regulus), whose mother is a lynx. In these fragmentary shards from Lucy's archaic and lyrical translation, he says to the star child:

> My heart is thee. Thou art my heart. Thy name is my heart . . . We do walk the sky . . . Therefore thou art a star child. Thou art red, for . . . thou resemblest me. Me, whose flesh red. Mother's flesh is different . . . mother walks the earth. I walk the sky . . . Thou must be the Day-Heart child. For, I give thee my name . . . I come out of the house, I walk behind thee in the sky. We must gently go. For, we are stars . . . Mother, mother becomes a lynx who must kill springbok, for mother's name must be lynx . . . For we do walk the sky. We must gently go above (in) the sky for, we are stars. Mother is a lynx, she eats springbok . . . Therefore we are stars. We must walk the sky; for we are heaven's things. Mother is earth's thing. She must walk the earth. She must sleeping lie the ground . . . we are stars which sleep not.[60]

Reading these words now, the intimate universe of persons and relationships that they evoke seems unattainably distant from our own. Perhaps this is why so many subsequent writers and artists who have studied, translated and interpreted the archive seem to have found its imagery of animals, stars and rain, images of longing and transcendence, impossible to resist. //Kabbo told the story of the Day-Heart Star and his child to Lucy over several weeks in mid-1872. It was winter, he was getting old, and he had been living in suburban Mowbray for around eighteen months. Increasingly, until about a year later, when he says directly that it is time to return home, his stories speak of home-sickness. Perhaps our readings of the archive now articulate a similar longing.

And if this is so, if the stories we tell about this past tell of our nostalgia for something that we feel has been lost, what can we learn from this desire?

The night is deep and wide. Animals are sleeping and hunting on the hills. The hills are made of stones and dreams and red sand. The hills are still and the great sky is rippled with patterns of banded cloud, thick with stars. A small town twinkles on the western horizon, Kathu perhaps, or Sishen. Tomorrow.

Who was here before us? How can we know? Together, standing in the cold, cold night, standing together in the cold, our breath is warm, like theirs. Our bodies touch, like theirs. Here in this place where our bodies touch, I feel their unextinguished warmth, small fire burning in the cold.

IMPALA

Wilderness may temporarily dwindle,
but wildness won't go away.

GARY SNYDER

Waking at dawn, going out into the cold, the world is rimmed with pink and blue. An impala doe nibbles leaves from an acacia tree a few steps from the chalet. Her tender tongue curls around the thorns and her downy chin moves as she chews. Two others are beside her, watching my stillness with dark eyes, their raised ears patterned like the veins of a leaf. Here among roads, chalets and parked city cars, the world is always watching.

For three million years or more impalas have come here at dawn to nibble the fragrant leaves. Older than tended fires and worked stone tools, the impala doe steps delicately among the trees, her soft nose and ears alert, at ease.

May the grace of her embodied mind endure in this place. May her children endure. May the sweetness of the living hills in the changing dawn endure, here in the dawn where everything changes.

On the hill behind the chalet something else is moving, someone who is the colour of the pale veld grass, walking. The buck grazes quietly in the dawn grass, treading among stone tools and discarded snake-skins. When he raises his head, his horns are long, antlers in fact. I wonder who he is, beautiful antlered person grazing on the morning hill.

Later, checking out of the lodge at Reception, I ask about him.

"Yes, it's what we call a takbok," the woman says.

"A reindeer?"

"Yes, a reindeer. The manager imported them."

"Why did he do that?"

"I don't know."

As we are leaving, we find that the little vervet monkey has followed us to the car. She jumps on the back window, looking in at the children. Seeing a bag of bananas, the monkey raises eyebrows and stares. The children touch hands with her through the glass, little fingerprints on either side, touching the glass.

"Oh, monkey!" they call. "Oh, sweet monkey!"

I start the car, drive slowly away.

IRONSTONE

The distinctive landmark for Kathu is an enormously huge truck and a monstrous digger parked beside the turn-off to the mining town. Originally used at the Sishen iron-ore mine, they have now been put on display for visitors to wonder at. The chunky proportions of wheel to body make the vehicles look like toys, but really they are gigantic.

Sophie and Sky are fascinated. "*Please* can we go and climb on them?"

"Yes, we will, on our way back from looking at the handaxes at the site. But before that we're going to do some shopping at Kathu, and then have a quick look at the mine."

The streets of Kathu, one of three modern residential areas built near Sishen to house its human resources, are broad and tree-lined, equipped with clinics and a hospital, as well as schools, businesses and fifty-one social and recreational clubs which cater for thirty-eight sports.

We find our way to Shoprite to get some provisions, and for the children to spend the money they have saved for the holiday. More starkly stereotyped than anything we have seen in Cape Town, the boys' toys are all guns and artillery, while those for girls are simply fashion and beauty. After long deliberation Sky buys a walkie-talkie with an indistinct recorded message. Sophie finds a silvery tiara Alice band and earrings, set with red, blue and green plastic jewels.

The nearby Sishen Mine is the origin of half the world's resources of lumpy iron ore. The brochure for the site informs the reader in deadly prose that open-pit methods are used for mining the high-grade haematite iron ore by an operation that employs about 3 000 people, that the mining company's steel plants consume about 6.8 million tons of Sishen's iron ore a year, and that the balance of the mine's production of about 27 million tons a year is exported. The daily maximum pit production capacity is 310 000 tons of ore and waste rock. The primary drilling is performed by electrically driven rotary drills, while crawler-mounted and rubber-wheeled compressor-air drills are used for secondary drilling. The average blast at Sishen frees, as they put it, roughly 250 000 tons of material. On 8 April 1981, a world record was set at the mine when 7.2 million tons of rock were broken during a single blast. Blasting efficiency at the mine is about 3.2 tons of rock per kilogram of explosives. According to the brochure, the mining is done in three eight-hour shifts by four teams of workers, seven days a week. All day, every day, they mine the site. One day the ore will all be used up.

We discover that one cannot actually visit the mine without making a booking, and that, anyway, the guides are all at a funeral. But driving as close as you are permitted to the guard-controlled entrance, you can see the mine trucks and steel structures in the distance and the great red dumps of pinkish-grey sand, haematite red, the colour of iron oxide.

From outside, the place does not seem quite the hellish and dreadful factory of Kali Yuga that I had expected. It simply looks enormous and unbeautiful – ordinary, industrial, efficient. But I know that out of sight the mine descends in Dantean layers to a depth of 375 metres, that the monster trucks far down appear like toys against the vast expanse of excavation, and that in time the open pit will eventually reach 12 kilometres across the territory, a great scar on the land 1.5 kilometres wide.

Feeling more comfortable with metaphors than with facts of this kind, I imagine the iron that is excavated from this mine being represented alchemically by the sign of Mars, a circle with a pointing arrow. The iron is hard and strong, enduring and unyielding. When a person is iron-hearted, when the iron enters his soul, this means that he is harsh, cruel, merciless, severe and unimpressionable. Steel is made from iron, but it is even harder, and it can be ground down to a fine sharp edge or point. A man or a woman of steel is hard and unbending, strong as steel, cold as steel, possessed of a mind that is cutting, indomitable and nerved for endurance.

After the long, long years of stone tools, human beings in the north discovered the technologies of metal: bronze and iron. The use of iron and copper, for hoes, spears and ornaments, was brought south to this region by farmers about two thousand years ago. They traded in metal work with their Khoe-San neighbours in the drier areas of the

Northern Cape, who otherwise continued to use tools of stone and wood and leather into the nineteenth century.

After this period came what may be called the recent age of industrial iron. This is an era marked by the use of tools, implements, weapons and machinery made of iron and steel: the nineteenth-century technologies of the Kimberley mine, the railway line and the train, the barrels of rifles, the bodies of military tanks, the gate at the entrance to Wonderwerk Cave and the barrier around the perimeter of the Kuruman Eye. Iron makes possible the wire fences on the farms, as well as sharp knives, saws, drills, nails, hammers, the steel engine of the car and all the other useful and dangerous engines that power our lives.

I read in the brochure that at Sishen the iron blood of the earth is drilled and broken and crushed and packed, to travel across the world to sixteen countries each year, constituting four per cent of the global seaborne iron-ore trade. So this is one of the very places where the iron and steel originate – and all the gleaming, pounding, shooting, slicing, whirring machineries of power from which they are forged.

At the entrance to the mine are notices advising workers on safety precautions in the workplace as well as warnings about HIV/Aids. Every visible surface is coated with a layer of fine red-grey dust. Everyone who works here must be breathing it in.

Not far from the mine and its town is Kathu Townlands, the place that was discovered as an archaeological site after graders from Sishen, digging for road gravel, unearthed a multitude of Stone Age tools.

This is the wonder that Duncan told us about in Cape Town and that Peter described at the museum. We park the car, get out, look around.

"Where are all the handaxes?" Sky wants to know.

Where indeed? The land is dry, an open field overgrown with grass. There are stones about, and, as elsewhere in the region, you can recognise one or two with a worked-off edge. But where are all the handaxes? I start to laugh. David said that we might find Kathu Townlands rather disappointing. Perhaps this is what he meant. How ironic if our pilgrimage or quest or treasure hunt into the heart of the land should discover at its destination just this dry place, and nothing special.

"I know we'll find it," Michael says. "We must just keep looking."

We cross to the other side of the road. Beyond the grass is a pile of rocks, banded ironstone. Yes. This must be it. The piles of stone extend into the veld as far as you can see. And here among the broken rocks are tools.

The tools lie simply on the ground, the ironstone tools, bands of red and black. We pick them up from where they lie: a cleaver, a handaxe, flakes and cores. The Earlier Stone Age tools crowd across the field in a gathering of silence – numberless stone artefacts, lying on the earth. Here is the place, not the story of the place. The day is hot, midday. The earth is red. The grasses are pale and full of insects. Cars go by on the road to Kathu. A bakkie pauses. The driver returns our wave, drives on.

This is where they came. They came to these rocks to make these tools. It is believed that the people who made the tools were a different species of *Homo* from ourselves. They were probably bigger people, different minds, yet still ancestral. And this is where they came, 600 000 years ago.

Down, down below stories, the silence of the place is big and deep. There are broken rocks and stone tools lying on the ground as far as you can see.

Peter Beaumont believes that the site extends across an area of about 0.5 x 3km, that it contains at least ten billion flaked items, and that they were probably produced during a fairly short period, perhaps one or two interglacials.[61] We walk and pick them up, hold the tools in our hands, put them on a rock to look at. Cleavers, cores, handaxes, worked-off stones, Acheulean things. The surface of the site has been so thoroughly overturned, first by the Sishen bulldozers and then presumably by archaeologists, that we will not be disturbing the stratigraphy by moving things around.

"Mommy!" says Sky suddenly, starting to cry. "You and Daddy and Sophie are finding them and not me."

"You'll find some, don't worry."

"But I want to go on the big truck! I want to go on the big truck now!"

"Okay, now look," I say, "you'll go on that truck, I promise you. But at the moment we're here. Kathu is a really special place. It's the place we travelled all this way to see. It's where they used to come to make the handaxes, very, very long ago. Maybe it's where they came to learn how to make them, like a sort of school, a workshop. Think of that. You *have* to give us all a chance to be here. I'll help you find some.

Afterwards we'll go to the truck. And you know what? Right now we're going to get some lunch."

Lost in the abundance of stone, I have to focus deliberately on each next step. Back to the car. Get out the picnic things. Carry them to a big rock, our table. Butter bread. Find cheese and tomatoes. A bottle of juice. Hand them out. Michael is roaming, picking up stones. Call him back for lunch. Sophie is moaning about thorns. Take off her shoes and socks, pick out all the prickles, put them on again. Sky has got prickles too, so take off his shoes and socks, pick out all the prickles, put them on again. Direct them both to somewhere in the grass to have a wee, where Sophie finds a snakeskin. Remind everyone to watch out for snakes. At last, with the family collected together in the eating of food, the children relax. Sophie puts on her new tiara, princess in the veld.

Sky says, "Why do archaeologists always take the best ones away?"

"Is that a riddle?" says Michael.

"I know, it's a pity, isn't it?" I say to Sky.

As Tony Humphreys told me before we left, archaeologists read the single copy of a precious book, and tear off pages as they read. In another metaphor, the excavation of a living environment attempts to form the various, sentient universe into a book, a text, an assemblage of words. And like the collecting nets of natural history or the machineries of the mine, the archaeological grid makes possible the naming and discipline of the earth, a plunder of that which is not yet discovered, accumulation of treasure in the storerooms of the world, emptying out the cave.

To Sky we try to explain that this is what tends to happen when a place becomes a site, how sometimes if you want to find out about a thing you have to change it, cut it up, dig into it. Then it's not what it was before. But if you hadn't tried to find out, if you hadn't dug the hole, or maybe taken the handaxes away to study, you would never know. It's like Wonderwerk Cave. It's all dug up now, but if they hadn't excavated it, nobody would know what was there. Nobody would know how wonderful it was.

"I wish they hadn't *done* that!" Sophie says indignantly. "It must have been so nice before, in that cave."

Sky says, "Well, it's nice, and it's not nice. Sort of, you want to eat your cake and have it."

But Sophie wants to know why they don't just put all that earth back in the cave.

"Yes," Sky agrees, "and where is it all now anyway?"

"In a storeroom somewhere, and in boxes in the museum," I say, "and of course most of it got scattered across farmlands, maybe in the Free State. The farmers thought it was fertiliser."

After lunch I tell the children, "I'm going to wander over that way a bit. You can stay here if you like, have some juice and chips."

Fed now and cared for, they seem happy enough with this arrangement and settle together companionably among a heap of stones, finding things and showing them to each other. Michael agrees to stay closer to the home base so that I can walk away.

Walking among the quiet multitude of stones and grasses, our feet tread among scattered tools and dust. More artefacts lie underground, hidden and buried, and we are walking over them. Arrived at last at this our destination, the mind struggles to find some hook of narrative or metaphor to which it might attach. But here there are no stories left, for the field is long since emptied of people or the comfort of language. Again, the land is stone and grass and dust.

Looking back, I can see the children absorbed in the particularity of the veld. Sophie is bending over, picking up handaxes. Sky is a small faded T-shirt and khaki hat in a sea of blond grasses, singing. As I walk away again among the scattered rocks which hold the markings of deep human time, my life is a trace of dust on the feet. Here, as they say, our flesh is grass, is dust.

And here, right now, deep below stories, there is a place where only rocks endure. The silence of the place is wide and empty, for stone tools do not speak. They do not speak of hands that are strong and warm, of people flaking, working, making things. The stones remember nothing of the blows that formed an edge. The stones are still. At midday in winter, the stones are warm. When dropped, the stones ring like iron. Already the grasses are growing over the recent excavations and the red sands blow in to cover up the traces of human habitation, layer on layer. In a few years the site could be quite invisible again.

Walking across the ironstone field, I know that the worked stone tools are emptied of words and story. Yet each particular one recalls the shaping form of human mind, this multitude of what we are. Our flesh is grass, is dust. And still the grasses grow, small seeds blown in the wind,

the myriad grasses of this veld. Walking among the long-forgotten Stone Age tools, among the tenacious communities of blond and green and reddish grass, remembering the ineradicable continuity of this seed, the scent of the veld is delicate and familiar.

Looking back, I can see the children now sitting on a rock, socks off, huddled together in the midday sun, cotton hats thrown to the ground, fair skins exposed. At my feet is one particularly fragrant plant whose name I do not know. Still here.

"Mommy! Mommy!" I can hear them shrilling from their perch on the rock. Now, as they watch me walking away and away among the stones, their cries become more and more insistent: "Mommy, come!"

I come.

"Look," Michael says, "a thing of beauty is a joy for ever."

He is holding in his hand the prepared ironstone blank for a handaxe in which each blow has opened up the banded layers, dark and pale. Each flake has made the rippled flow. It is like the master handaxe in the museum, but rougher, incomplete, probably cast aside. I show him a smaller one, mottled with white. It looks like a heart, the rounded form shaped to a point.

"It's unspeakable," I say clumsily, "so big and quiet. It's impossible to grasp the experience."

"Yes, it is. But what you *can* do is to experience the grasp. Hold the tool in your hand, feel what they felt. The tools still talk to the hand after all these years."

Holding the small stone heart, I can feel that the stone is warm at midday. My warm hand holds the small warm heart, heart which other hands have made, hard cutting edge held in this hand. Tool or weapon, the fine worked edge still carries across the generations the wordless grasp of human agency and the form of the mind's intention. Holding it in my hand, I feel a sort of tenderness towards the mindful hands that made it first and held it, knew its symmetry, its weight and form. This is the feel of an artefact in the hand, this thing we do.

"Look, Mommy!" Sophie calls. "A beautiful butterfly, black and yellow, with a purple spot!"

"Mommy, look!" says Sky. "I found a stone that looks like a mountain."

We help them put on shoes and socks again and gather up the picnic.

Michael photographs the pile of tools we have assembled on the rock. Then we each take a few stones and scatter them back in the veld, say thank you to the ancestors.

Leaving, I do not want to leave. If only there were something I could take back home to help me remember the veld and the dust and stones and colours and silence of Kathu, even some small shard, some piece of stone that has not been worked, a photograph of grass. Searching among the fragments at our feet, we cannot at first find even a single bit of stone that shows no signs of human culture. Then at last I pick up something to take without dilemma, a broken piece of banded ironstone, layered and layered, dark and red, unworked.

Getting back into the car, I notice for the first time the melons growing by the side of the road, foraging food. The children remind us of the San tale about the elephant who died during a drought so that his body could become fruit and melons and grasses for the other animals to eat.

Our final stop in the area is the unavoidable monster trucks near the turn-off to Kathu. Michael and I stay in the car while the children dash off to climb up high on one of the big steel Sishen vehicles, too high for me to watch. I look away to read the map of Kathu on the tourist signboard.

Aside from the mine, the landmarks it indicates are the standard ones for a small South African town, signposted here mostly in Afrikaans, but with a few intriguing concessions to English speakers: "Golf Course, Sportgronde, Hospitaal, Civic Centre, Polisie, Hoërskool, Primary School, Post Office, Kettingwinkel, Steakhouse, Motorhawe, Winkels,

Videos, Banke, Kafees, Apteke, Informasie, Natuur Reservaat" and so on. Around the map is a patchwork of advertisements: "Kathu Bande, Kathu Kafee, Slaghuis Vleismark, TV Rama Toys and Pets, Mokala Safari Adventures". Across the road another sign depicts a gemsbok, distinctive icon of the region, and the words: "Sishen Iron Ore Mine/We serve the community/We support the fight against HIV and Aids". Nowhere on the Kathu visitors' signs, nor in any of the tourist information for the region, is any mention made of its archaeological treasure. Kathu Townlands remains invisible, unseen in the midst.

Looking back to the truck, I see that the children are very little and the vehicles are very big. A plaintive voice calls from high up on one of them: "What are we going to do to get down? It was so terrifying coming up."

Michael goes over to help, and I am glad to see the twins climbing down. They run to the car, carrying brochures about iron ore and Sishen that they got from the tourist office inside the digger. The mine apparently has an expected life of another forty years before the iron will be all mined out. It sounds like a long time. The directors of the company, the shareholders, the overseas clients, the workers and administrators will all be dead or pretty old by then. It sounds like a long time, forty years.

Michael walks over and calls me out of the car: "Come, there's something I want you to have a look at."

On the white enamel painted hubcap of the biggest truck tyre, a visitor has written these words with a permanent black marker:

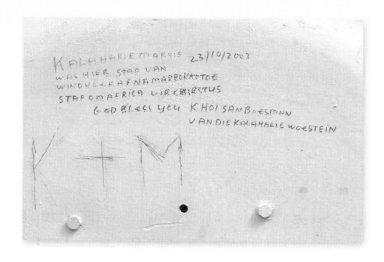

KALAHARIE margis 23/10/2003
was HIER staan VAN
windhoek AFNAmaskokattoe
staan om AFRICA vir CHRISTUS
God Bless you KHOI SAN Boesman
VAN DIE KALAHARIE woestein

K + M

Humans can walk long distances. I wonder how far this one has now travelled on his quest. In the course of our particular journey through the region, I have seen my life as a millimetre of dust in the cave. The recent industrial period and all of recorded history measure just a little more. Beyond and beneath, the layers of deep dust accumulate among shards of bone and stone and grass bedding layers, the pulse of ice ages, cooling and warming of the earth, dust of their feet through all the generations down, all the way down to the soft ash of the fires, a million years down.

Below the inscription on the Sishen digger's wheel, the initials "K" and "M" scratched through the white paint reveal streaks of the steel beneath, already rusting red.

Not far from this, at Kathu Townlands, whether or not we know or care or understand, the Stone Age tools reside, undecayed in hundreds of thousands of years. Cars pass by, grasses grow, and the fine dust of aeolian sands blows in from the Kalahari. Here in the midst of all our words and fears and the iron machineries of the present dispensation, the field of wordless artefacts remains. Overgrown with grasses, hidden from view, the myriad stones of human mind endure, right here in the midst.

STARS

The last site we are visiting on the way back to Kimberley is a specularite mine near Postmasburg called Blinkklipkop. We have not seen specularite before but understand that it is a crystalline form of haematite. This makes it iron oxide, like the great deposit of iron ore at Sishen, but instead of being dense and hard, it is composed of tiny flakes that glitter, mirrors or specula that reflect the light.

For people who lived here before the age of iron and even for many of them afterwards, the shimmering substance was something precious. Blinkklipkop, the place is called, shining stone hill. In Tswana the name is Tsantsabane, which Burchell and others turned into Sensavan. It is also called Sibihlong, the place of sibilo, specularite. In /Xam the word for specularite is //hara.

South of Kathu, near a signpost to the Lohatla Army Battle School, we pass a collection of little houses made of branches, broken-off bushes and some tarpaulins and plastic. I imagine that the poignant shelters grouped together on the side of the road are the homes of karretjie-mense, the sheep-shearing descendants of the KhoeKhoen and /Xam-speaking San, whose communities were destroyed by colonial invasions. After the genocide, the remaining so-called tame Bushmen usually became farm labourers. Within a few generations, the introduction of wire fencing, among other things, meant that many had to leave the farms, since shepherds were no longer needed.

Research by Michael de Jongh on the karretjiemense describes them as the poorest of the poor, people of no fixed abode who are strangers everywhere they go, people living well below any of the recognised measures of absolute poverty, people whom all the benefits of place have eluded.[62] Dispossessed of land, they travel from farm to farm during the shearing season, shearing the sheep. Home is a donkey karretjie and the small low shelters that they build on the side of the road from plastic and corrugated iron, sometimes structured around the cart itself like a nest made of grass, a house made of reeds and stones, a temporary shelter on the road. Like //Kabbo and the other prisoners at the Breakwater Lodge, they are often described by farmers as sheep-stealers, Karretjie-Boesmans. A man looks out as our car flashes by.

At Postmasburg we stop for more provisions and immediately a child in dirty rags with a bruise below his right eye is begging at the window of the car.

"No, sorry," I say, "I don't give money."

Michael says, "I wonder whose descendants they are."

I pass the boy some biscuits to share with his friends.

Off the tar, the dirt road winds among dry farms, turning off near two hills that David has told us to look out for. A small, battered sign indicates "Caves/Grotte". We park the car and walk past the farmhouse with its line of washing, rusty iron tanks and the inevitable barking dogs.

Across a dip in the veld, then up to a small koppie, the mine is a strange dark hole against the hill. It seems to have been excavated from grey rock the colour of graphite, and another reddish rock that is soft to the touch. The red comes off on our hands, and I realise that it is ochre, ttò, the oldest pigment, haematite in another form.

Sky shouts, "Look! The rocks are twinkling!"

Suddenly in daylight, stars shimmer at our feet like tiny diamonds.

"It's like walking in fairyland," Sophie says, wondering.

Swallows' nests have been built against the excavated roof, and bats fly out at us, one of them white. A deep, old smell of dassies fills the mine, and I wonder how many generations of dassie piss have hardened in resinous accumulations on the rocks.

Human animals at least have been coming to Blinkklipkop for an incredibly long time. When Peter Beaumont and others excavated the site, they found battered stones that had been used for mining, as well as pieces of decorated pottery, pieces of ostrich eggshell and animal bone. From these they concluded that people with domesticated sheep and goats were mining the hill and using ceramics here from around 1 200 years ago.

But members of our species were here way before this. As Peter told us in Kimberley, traces of specularite have been found at Canteen Kopje in a level thought to be about 350 000 years old. The site is 200 kilometres away from this mine, which is a very great distance to travel for something you can neither eat nor wear nor use for tools or shelter. In this sense the shimmering specularite is like ochre, or like the quartz crystals and chalcedony excavated at Wonderwerk Cave. The Later Stone Age burial at Peers' Cave of the young woman garlanded with beads and crystals, her body rubbed with pigments, is something wonderful. But to discover such things so deep down in the archaeological record is quite extraordinary. It suggests how very long ago our ancestors loved beautiful things or reached for loveliness beyond immediate need or use. How long we have sought for something radiant, colourful, magical, we might now call it spiritual, a kind of treasure.

In recent history the use of specularite is quite well documented. William Burchell described in 1811 how Tswana people would barter ironware of their own manufacture – knives, assegais and hatchets, as well as tobacco, copper bracelets and ornaments for the ears – in exchange for porcelain beads and sibilo.[63] Then, in 1835, John Campbell noted that what he calls Blink Mountain is a kind of Mecca to the nations around, who are constantly making pilgrimages to it to obtain fresh supplies of the blue shining powder and the red stone.[64]

Burchell's story of the use of specularite by BaTlhaping is told with some irony:

> The mode of preparing and using it, is simply grinding it together with grease, and smearing it generally over the body, but

chiefly on the head; and the hair is so much loaded and clotted with an accumulation of it, that the clots exhibit the appearance of lumps of mineral. A Bachapin whose head is thus covered, considers himself as most admirably adorned, and in full dress.[65]

Fifty years later, /Han≠kass'o's explanation to Lucy Lloyd of the treasures of ttò and //hara describes in a different tone a similar procedure:

> //hara is that which is black; people (having mixed it with fat) anoint their head with it, while ttò is red, and people rub their flesh with it; when they have pounded it; they pound it, pound it, pound it, they rub their flesh with it. They pound //hara; they anoint their heads, while they have first pounded ttò; they first rub their flesh with ttò. And they pound //hara, they anoint their heads. [66]

In Kimberley David told us that Later Stone Age burials which he and others have excavated in the Northern Cape often contain specularite, usually traces on the cranium, and sometimes a collection of //hara or sibilo sealed in an ostrich-egg container. As /Han≠kass'o said to Lucy Lloyd:

> //hara sparkles, therefore our heads shimmer on account of it; while they feel that they sparkle, they shimmer. Therefore the

Bushmen are wont to say, when the old women are talking there: "That man, he is a handsome young man, on account of his head, which is surpassingly beautiful with the //hara's blackness."[67]

Now Sophie rubs ochre on her face and Sky puts some on her hands and on his. They find a little cavern where he can easily dig out some silvery grey specularite, rub it on hands and feet, rub it in our hair. We clap hands, the children and I, and the air fills with drifting stars.

It has been said that a young man's head adorned with //hara is like a great tree, covered in berries. His head shimmers like water in the sunlight, for when the sun is above the water, you can see underneath the sun how the water shimmers. Now the children's small pale hands are silver, their cheeks are ochre, and there is an unearthly expression in their eyes. Clapping our hands, we are playing with the stars, the shimmering of sun across the water. Like water in sunlight, like stars in the stream, like a silver fire, this shimmering. Like blood, this old red stain of ochre on the skin.

Suddenly I realise that Michael seems to be restless, watching, not getting involved. When I ask, he says he feels uncomfortable, as though he is in a place where he doesn't really belong.

His disquiet makes me pause, look around, see the darkness of the hollowed-out hill. Perhaps the children and I have been silly, insensitive, too light and blithe in response to the uncanny resonance of the mine. /Han≠kass'o told Lucy Lloyd that people are afraid when they go to the mountain where the //hara and ttò are mined. He said people feel that sorcerers live there, that they make their houses there in small holes, like mouse holes. He does not seem to have visited this place himself, but he knows that people throw stones at the mine when they come there to get //hara and ttò. For they want the sorcerers that inhabit the mine to hide themselves. That is why they throw stones.[68]

Certainly there is a strangeness at Blinkklipkop, but I do not think we need to be afraid. Michael starts taking photographs, and I interpret this to mean that he is happy, or at least resigned to stay a bit longer. It is already late afternoon and the sun is getting low.

Sky says, "Well, I *do* feel at home here," and continues playing.

Though people have been coming to this mine for hundreds of thousands of years, the tiny mirrors in the stone still twinkle. Rub soft iron starlight on skin and see the insubstantial, delicate shimmering, like sunlight on the water, like fires in the dark, rare crystals of stardust falling through the air, mirror flakes caught in the last light of the day. Rub it on skin and on hair, and know the body adorned with //hara in life and death, stars packed into the head for burial, cranium encrusted with specularite, head wrapped with stars for the long voyage into night, the night sky thick with stars, journeying into the radiant star field, water shimmering in the sun, light as stars, old as joy. For once you have seen the stars, you know that – what is it you know? Once you have seen the stars . . . We are the stars, says the Day's Heart to his child. We are the sky's things. We must walk the sky.

Near the entrance of the cave is the bank of red ochre. This soft iron ore has been in human use for possibly 400 000 years or more. Red pigment ground into fine powder and used for painting animals and people, mixed with fat and fragrant herbs, rubbed into leather and on living bodies, and buried with the dead. Imagining now some ancestral ritual act, I rub a streak of ttò on my cheeks and feel the warmth of redness on my skin on this cold afternoon, touch of soft iron pigment on the face, red as earth, red as ochre, warm as blood, old as fire, warm heart of our body, remembering.

"Wouldn't you say that ochre and specularite are more special than face-paints and the glitter you get in shops?" I ask the children.

I am thinking of the face-painting clowns at fairs and birthday parties in Cape Town, and of the many forms in which the toy industry markets glitter, glitter pens, glitter glue, and all the paraphernalia of fairies.

"Oh, it's *much much* more special. It's treasure."

As we leave the mine, our skin is shimmering and ochre-red, as though the stars and earth have marked this modern skin like poems of our inheritance.

On the long way back to Kimberley the day fades into a night that is dark and full of more stars. When at last the big lights appear on the horizon to mark our destination, the jewelled lights of the city that sparkles are set like manufactured stars laid out in grids across the night, burning. At the edge of this strange luminescence we pass an unelectrified village of little houses made of corrugated iron and bits of plastic.

"Look at their fires," someone says, "burning outside in the dark."

"Do you think they're cold, the poor people?" Sky asks.

"I should think so."

"Do you think they're better or worse off than the San?" Michael wonders.

It is easy for us, of course, to regret the loss of a life of hunting and gathering, unpropertied and free. It must have been different and more difficult in numerous particular ways from what we can envisage now, looking back. Yet when cold shelters huddle on the side of the road outside an army base, and skeletons lie heaped into graves, and people live in shacks at the edges of a city built on the excavation of treasure, is this not a story of loss?

Driving through Kimberley, we pass the stone Siege Memorial. On the steps, as though staged deliberately to intervene at this point in the narrative, a group of six people are having an alfresco dinner, dressed in formal cream suits and long dresses that are reminiscent of an earlier time. The table is lit with candles and laid with a white cloth. Someone is playing a guitar. The men are wearing pith helmets.

As we approach Gum Tree Lodge, the children remind us that they have waited a long time to see the puppy. As soon as we arrive, they dash next door to say hello and the puppy's owners kindly let them stay.

Later David comes to visit and to say goodbye.

"How's it going with the burials?"

"Slowly. We found a coffin yesterday, collapsed, with the pelvic bones sticking through. The skull had a halo of splintered wood, really macabre."

He describes the precise, attentive, almost contemplative awareness that is involved in their excavation, and talks about the bones of young people, fractured, punctured and burnt. He says that in one grave a broken head had been tied together with electrical cord, and that in others there were severed limbs, extra ones, tossed in with someone else.

He says that he is beginning to believe that the graves do not in fact relate to some single event, like a mining accident, a fire, the Siege, the Flu. Instead, it seems most likely that they represent what one might call "ordinary time" in Kimberley in the late nineteenth century, a fast developing town which then had the highest mortality rates in the country. They were probably black people from out of town, he says, mostly young men. But there are also some women, a toddler and a stillborn baby. If you were black and a migrant, the city that sparkles was a place of iron machineries and dust, of mining compounds and hospital compounds, disease and danger, and people heaped together in graves, without record or ceremony. Most of them died from mal-nutrition.

I ask him the same question I asked when we first met at the Gladstone burial ground: "What really happens, do you think, when a place becomes a site? You know, when the ground is marked up with grids for excavation?"

He ponders a bit and then says: "I have come to believe that excavation ought always to be more than a little harrowing for the practitioner. The act is a dismantling that is nonreversible, and not every aspect is readily captured. Some of what you find is impossible to bag."

And then, as though this were unusual, he adds, "The skeletons are getting into our dreams."[69]

We tell him about the places we visited in the Kuruman area.

He says, "I don't really like the word 'cosmetics' for ochre and specularite. I think it was something more than that."

"Yes, it sounds trivial, which it isn't at all. Why did you say we might be disappointed at Kathu?"

"Well, I didn't know how . . . to what extent you could . . ."

"Whether we would see them?"

"Yes. The site isn't as self-evident as Wonderwerk. You have to know what you're looking for."

"Now that we've been there, Peter's claims don't seem that incredible."

"No, they don't. It's vast."[70]

I ask him about the shelters outside Postmasburg: "Are they karretjie-mense?"

"Actually, they're not," he says. "It's a totally different history, but an interesting one. They're members of the Tswana community who were ejected from Maremane/Ga-Tlhose as part of homeland consolidation and to make way for the army base there, the Lohatla Army Battle School – you probably saw the sign."

"Yes, we did."

"Well, the people have naturally been putting in a land claim since '94. But the Battle School is strategic, and so on, so they haven't been successful. As a form of protest some of the community have set up camp outside the entrance to 'their' land. They toyi-toyi sometimes, and I think the road has been blocked once or twice."

We talk and talk, not wanting the journey to be over.

When David has gone and I close my eyes to sleep, the visual field of burning stars is filled with cleavers and handaxes, the old flaked edge of lithic forms. All night I dream about stones.

HOME

There is another route back to Cape Town via Upington, which passes through /Xam-ka !au, the home territory of //Kabbo, Dia!kwain and the other informants. This is the land of the Flat Bushmen and the Grass Bushmen, where Janette Deacon tracked down the pans and koppies and sweet grasslands that they described in the archive, and found her way to the farm where old man Hendrik Goud still knew some last words of the /Xam language.

But it is a long slow route to anywhere on that road now, crows eating a bat-eared fox on the hot tarmac, the vast fields bleak and flat and dry, and the sheep-farmed land cropped bare of people and springbok. At the town of Kenhardt, not far from where Dia!kwain was shot dead by farmers soon after his return from Cape Town, a sign announces "Rock Art B&B", and at Brandvlei you can buy poor-quality fake Bushman crafts at the tiny roadside café. We encounter these things on a later trip, but this time we have chosen to return home the way we came.

Getting into the car at Gum Tree Lodge, Sky says, "Sophie, I'm going to give you three wishes. You can wish for anything: a puppy or a control helicopter. Or you can wish for real wings that fly, or that the world was back to wildness again."

She knows the answer immediately: "I'm going to wish for a puppy."

"Okay, I'll get you a puppy. Do you want a sausage dog?"

"Yes."

"What about the wings?"

"I'll have the wings too."

As we leave Kimberley in the grey cold light before dawn, the golden lemons gleam in the headlights. A little fire burns on the roadside, lighting up a thin man seated on an upturned tin. Outside the city a big sign advertises "Stone Crushers: Crushed Stone and Sand". There is always someone digging a hole and dumping the rubble.

Sophie counts telephone poles, aloud. She stops at eight hundred. Sky counts the cellphone aerials or pawks. He stops at forty.

Some of the telephone poles are scaffolding for sociable weavers' nests – the giant teddy, the bear hive, the bulky bird and many others. The ornithologist Mark Anderson (who told me about the flamingos at Kamfersdam) and other researchers have described in a scientific paper their observation of twenty-five sociable weaver colony sites over a period of eight years. This work has shown that while the weavers' nest can house as few as twenty and as many as five hundred birds in one colony, those living in the larger groups have a better rate of survival. The research method involved a group of people capturing large numbers of the birds at regular intervals into mist nets at dawn. They would then take them out of the nets, and put each one into a linen bag in order to label it with a ring around the leg. Finally the birds were all released.[71]

Driving home from dawn to dusk again, our bodies are held in the turbulent space of the car, together with the journey's accumulation of stones, dust, chocolate digestives, children's tapes, animals, books and bags of clothes. The first stop is Strydenburg, for petrol and for Sky to buy something for himself and his sister with his purseful of coppers. In the tiny shop near the garage his little hands spread a pile of small change before the woman behind the counter. But her tough face does not smile.

"Ons vat nie meer vyfsente nie," she says.

She does not smile to see the pale star-shaped hands give her what he has, a heap of coins saved and counted, over and over for days.

"Ons moet dit alles terugstuur na die bank," she continues, her mouth set hard. "You must have it changed."

I find some coins, pay for the small sweet he bought to share, pour the money back into his purse, and steer him out of the shop.

Back in the car, we tell the story to the others, feeling hurt. She refused to take his money. Isn't that illegal? What was it about? On the fast modern road, all but the newest road signs have been used for shooting practice.

Hours later, passing through Leeu Gamka, we point out the ostrich farm to the children.

"Look, big prehistoric birds, hundreds of living dinosaurs. They should have the whole veld to run in, but the farmer has crammed them into that yard like chickens in one of those chicken factories. Can you see how grey the earth is? There's nothing left growing."

"Poor ostriches," they say appropriately.

At Laingsburg we stop again for petrol. Although I do remember the Gladstone skeletons and the lesson of their perfect teeth, I take Sophie and Sky into a shop for a last sweet treat before home. What they choose costs twenty cents each. This time, when the coppers are poured out from their purses, the woman smiles. One child at a time, she helps them count out twenty one-cent pieces.

"That's fine," she says, "we're always glad to have the change."

More hours on, we enter the Hex River Valley, threshold of the damper, moister Western Cape. When Mary Elizabeth Barber arrived here on her long journey from Kimberley to Cape Town, she described the farmlands as a little paradise amongst the mountains, and remarked on the extraordinary size of their grapes. In particular, though, she marvelled at the engineering skill of the men who built the railway through the mountains, and she saw this steel construction as an enduring landmark for generations to come. Like the stone tools she observed in the Northern Cape, this work of nineteenth-century endeavour seemed to her an artefact that would hold its form unchanged by time. "All is rock, solid rock," she wrote, "and ages hence this railroad will be as it is today."[72]

Returning from our lithic quest, we do not much notice the railway line. But the mountains themselves resemble handaxes and scrapers, the worked-off edges of massive tools. On the side of the road, the labourers still stand holding out boxes of late, sweet grapes. And in the afternoon light the colours of the vineyards gleam red and gold. Like Mary Barber, we find them beautiful, this bright patchwork grid of cultivation.

Suddenly Sky says, "I want to go back! I want to go back right now to Kimberley." He is sobbing, angry. "You're going to stop the car and turn around and go back. Did you hear what I said?"

Driving on, we tell him that home is good too, and that he'll be happy to be there. But I feel my reassurances lack conviction. Travelling back towards the city, I remember the tender mouth of an impala doe chewing leaves in the early dawn. I remember a valley of Kalahari trees and red sand, and a small child drawing patterns in the dust. I remember clear water and stars, the hill above Wonderwerk Cave and the enduring silence of the stones. If the ancient cave is home, then the wild hills are familiar, and our ancestors' bodies are gone into that very neighbourhood, swallows flying, mice and weeds. My heart hurts and, like Sky, I want to stop the car at once, go back to where we came from.

Still, we drive on relentlessly. At last he is soothed by the reminder of the piano that is waiting at home for him to play. I try to find some comfort in remembering that the sadness I feel is not something new, that since childhood I have been afraid that loss might be irrevocable, afraid of walking out of the Garden and being unable to return.

As we arrive in Cape Town, the city lights are coming on again in the twilight. In our Muizenberg street the neighbours are waiting for us with smiles and a box of organic vegetables. Yet, still my heart hurts.

The sun is just setting as we open up the house. Once we have unloaded the car, Michael takes me up to the balcony and points to the pink and orange clouds on the horizon, the changing light of dusk on the mountains: "Look."

I allow myself then to see the colours of the evening, and recognise the kindness of his reminder. My heart still feels sad, but I am beginning to let it go.

After supper Sophie sits down to look at the treasures she keeps beside her bed in the engraved brass box that was my father's. She takes out each one carefully: a shimmering porcelain unicorn, a tiny glass seal from Italy, a yellow button she picked up on the beach, a piece of rose quartz, a little brass dog. As always, she tells the story of each particular precious thing, laying them out in a row. When she is done, each one is put back in its place.

"I like to be neat," she says. "I like to put them back in order."

Now there are crystals, stones and pieces of agate from the desert to add to her collection. I watch her ordering her world again, mind recollecting, making sense.

Still looking for something more, a little restless, I find a recording of *The Trout Quintet* from among our disordered collection of CDs and put it on to play. Remembering how my father taught me to listen to this particular piece of music, I tell the children to wait for the trout in the Fourth Movement. Listen to its song, dancing up the stream in the rippling light. Listen to how it repeats and changes. Listen to the river, Tema con variationi.

Later Sky lights candles and sits us all down for a concert, his small face radiant in the candlelight as he plays my father's piano. We listen and clap, recollecting these familiar things, treasures of home.

HEARTH

On the first night back I dream of Grandad, my father's father, now twenty years dead. Michael and I are visiting him and discover that he has a collection of handaxes and other lithic artefacts that we have never known about. Among the papers and pens on his desk are also some stones he has kept because they are beautiful, just stones picked up in the veld. In the dream his study is compelling, a writer's room, a historian's, a place for things he finds important.

Waking, I remember that when Batista Salvador spoke about healing, he said that if you visit the old places with a problem, your ancestors will come to you in a dream, show you what is happening. Tell you what to do.

Perhaps this is why I am now reminded that my grandfather studied botany and natural history at university, and that during his lifetime he planted many trees. I remember that he loved the plants that grew wild in the Natal veld, especially, for some reason, cabbage trees, and that on Sundays after church, which he never attended, he used to send the schoolboys out to explore the hills around Estcourt. The dream recalls that he enjoyed telling stories and that he was a writer who tried to interpret the past with integrity. Meeting my ancestor in the dream, Grandad, the founding patriarch of our family, domestic emblem of the Empire, I recognise now our continuity.

A few days later when we are driving to visit my mother, one of the children asks what would have happened if Granny's mother or her grandmother had never been born, or if Daddy's grandmother had died before she had had children.

I say, "Well, we wouldn't be around now."

It's like a big tree, I tell them. If you cut one of the branches, then all the other twigs and branches growing from it are gone too. People sometimes talk about a family tree in that way, a big spreading tree, with everyone connected.

Sophie asks, "Are we the trunk, Sky and me?"

"I think you're more like the little branches of the tree, the new green leaves, the buds at the tip. The tree itself goes back and back."

"All the way back to Wonderwerk Cave," says Sky.

"Yes, all the way back to that cave, and others, and even before that. It's a long, long, long way back. Maybe the trunk and the roots are all those ancestors, growing into the world. Or maybe the trunk of the tree is the world itself, and we are the branches. Or maybe it's all like grass, sprouting everywhere across the land without a beginning or an end. Do you remember all the grasses and plants at Wonderwerk, and the trees, and walking on the hill?"

"Yes, of course we remember." They are tired now of the conversation.

At home, the stones collect around the laptop on my desk. A little agate. A piece of jasper. A handaxe from the game lodge. Two pieces of banded ironstone from Kathu Townlands. Some white quartz from the dinosaur farm, marked with black lichen and red earth. A piece of jasper from the side of the road.

There are also some pieces of specularite and ochre from Blinkklipkop, //hara and ttò, which I should probably not have taken. But these things recollect an old longing and are difficult to resist, traces of red and of starlight on the skin. David told me that as recently as the 1950s Tswana people would come to the McGregor Museum to ask for sibilo, for specularite. They knew that the building housed a store of treasure, the shimmering of sun on water, ancestral heads packed with deep stars for burial, the beautiful bodies of young men adorned with the glittering dark.

At Wonderwerk Cave you can stand at the steel railing and look far down into the pit to where, unearthed by the trowels and other instruments of excavation, the ash from the early fires remains, a million years old or more. The swallows still nest against the fire-blackened roof, but the hearth is out, and the home floor is destroyed.

Back in the city we receive more and more frequent evidence that the present fires of human progress are spreading out of control. The carbon released by this conflagration is accumulating in the atmosphere, and the climate is changing. At home we have put in a solar geyser, but we still drive cars and leave on too many lights.

One evening while making supper Michael says he has an idea. It is the sort of idea that a poet or a craftsman might conceive after visiting the cave and sensing the tread of generations on the heart.

"The fire at Wonderwerk must be relit," he says emphatically. "First the archaeologists should backfill a good part of the excavation to restore the floor. And when they're finished the fire must be lit in the cave again."

Perhaps in this way the fire which was extinguished during the twentieth century might become a hearth once more, and people could visit from around the world, tending it in turns. Perhaps for those who came, the keeping of a small fire in the cave again might constitute some rite of recognition and remembering. Call it a sacred site, or a metaphor, or a place in which to witness the burning world, and to observe the practice of our original mind.

SOURCES

The extraordinary Bleek-Lloyd Collection has been a continuing inspiration in my work on this book. Soon after I read the actual notebooks, the archive became electronically available to anyone in the world who is linked into the global communication system of the Internet. So you can now ask Google about Bleek or Lloyd or /Xam and be taken to http://www.lloydbleekcollection.uct.ac.za, a website produced by Pippa Skotnes and Eustacia Riley, which brings together for the first time the Bleek and Lloyd collections from the archives of the National Library, Iziko, and the University of Cape Town. Skotnes has subsequently also published *Claim to the Country: The Archive of Wilhelm Bleek and Lucy Lloyd* (Johannesburg, Cape Town and Athens: Jacana and Ohio University Press, 2007), which includes a DVD of the *Digital Bleek and Lloyd*, another excellent resource.

Other primary works that have directly informed this project include Mary Barber's "Wanderings in South Africa by Sea and Land, 1879", published in *Quarterly Bulletin of the South African Library*, Vol 17.2 (1962) and Vol 17.3 (1963); Gary Snyder's *The Practice of the Wild: Essays by Gary Snyder* (San Francisco: North Point Press, 1990); and *Moon in a Dewdrop: Writings of Zen Master Dōgen* (ed. Kazuaki Tanahashi, San Francisco: North Point Press, 1985).

With regard to archaeology, the following have been particularly instructive: *Guide to Archaeological Sites in the Northern Cape* (Kimberley: McGregor Museum, 1990) and *Archaeology in the Northern Cape: Some Key Sites* (Kimberley: McGregor Museum, 2004), both compiled by Peter Beaumont and David Morris; Hillary and Janette Deacon's *Human Beginnings in South Africa: Uncovering the Secrets of the Stone Age* (Cape Town: David Philip, 1999); Nick Shepherd's various analyses of the discipline of archaeology in South Africa (for example "Disciplining Archaeol-sogy: The Invention of South African Prehistory, 1923-1953", *Kronos* 28 (2002), 127-145); and David Morris's MA thesis *Driekopseiland and "The Rain's Magic Power": History and Landscape in a New Interpretation of a Northern Cape Rock Engraving Site* (University of the Western Cape, 2002).

Here are some more particular notes about sources:

1 Bertie Peers, "Ancient Fish Hoek Man and his Home" in Malcolm Cobern, *The Story of the Fish Hoek Valley* (Fish Hoek: Published by the author, 1984), 16-26.

2 Questions of naming remain contested and unresolved. Unless the context requires "Bushman", I generally use the term "San" in the pages that follow, with "Khoe-San" as a collective term for various precolonial groups of foragers, hunters with sheep, and herders.

3 WG Sebald, *The Rings of Saturn* (London: Vintage, 2002), 170.

4 This fine work has since been published as *Bushmen in a Victorian World: The Remarkable Story of the Bleek-Lloyd Collection of Bushman Folklore* (Cape Town: Double Storey, 2006). Andrew's particular achievement, I think, is to have presented an accessible, meticulously researched and historically informative account of the lives and interactions of all the main individuals involved in the Bleek-Lloyd recording project. He comments in conclusion on the significance of the Collection: "First, it is the only record that we have of a culture that was practised in southern Africa for tens of thousands of years before the arrival of settlers or researchers from Europe. [. . .] Second, the collaboration between the researchers and the informants that made this salvaging operation possible provides an extraordinary tale not only of survival and resilience, but of hope and creative possibility. [. . .] Without romanticising the motivations of the researchers or the life histories of the informants, we can recognise that their ability to sustain a decade of dialogue is without precedent in the history of this country and perhaps that of the world" (397).

5 In what follows, the abbreviation "BC 151" refers to the Bleek Collection, Manuscripts and Archives Department, University of Cape Town. Materials recorded

by Wilhelm Bleek are classified as A1, and those recorded by Lucy Lloyd and Jemima Bleek as A2. In this case, for example, Adam Kleinhardt's words are referenced as: BC 151, A1.4.1.

6   BC 151, A2.1.44, 3481. Lloyd's use of the term "flints" is a little misleading, since flint itself is not found in the region.

7   BC 151, A2.1.101, 8314.

8   See Andrew Bank, "From Pictures to Performance: Early Learning at the Hill", *Kronos*, 28 (2002), 66-101.

9   BC 151, A2.1.79, 6365v.

10 BC 151, A2.1.105, 8560v.

11 Janette has discussed the representation of these places in detail in "My Place is the Bitterpits: The Home Territory of Bleek and Lloyd's /Xam San Informants", *African Studies*, 45 (1986), 135-155, and in "The Power of a Place in Understanding Southern San Rock Engravings", *World Archaeology*, Vol 20 No 1 (1988), 129-140. Her beautiful recent book about /Xam-ka !au is called *My Heart Stands in the Hill* (Cape Town: Struik, 2005) and is a collaboration with the photographer Craig Foster.

12 BC 151, A2.1.89, 7226v.

13 The question of the relative complicity of imperial travellers in the practices of colonial conquest and exploitation is discussed by Mary Louise Pratt in *Imperial Eyes: Travel Writing and Transculturation* (London: Routledge, 1992). In response to her analysis, William Beinart has convincingly shown that the writings of enlightenment scientific travellers were far less homogeneous than Pratt suggests. See his article: "Men, Science, Travel and Nature in the Eighteenth- and Nineteenth-Century Cape", *Journal of Southern African Studies*, Vol 24 No 4 (1998), 775-799.

14 Mary Elizabeth Barber, "Wanderings in South Africa by Sea and Land, 1879", *Quarterly Bulletin of the South African Library*, Vol 17.2 (1962), 45.

15 My comments on Mary Elizabeth Barber here and in subsequent chapters draw to some extent on two useful analyses of her role in colonial science. Firstly, in the article noted previously, William Beinart considers her work in natural his-

tory in the context of a discussion of the writings of some visiting male scientific travellers at the Cape, especially Anders Sparrman and William Burchell. Secondly, Alan Cohen discusses her involvement in the natural sciences but is more centrally concerned with her research into geology and prehistory. See "Mary Elizabeth Barber, the Bowkers, and South African Prehistory", *South African Archaeological Bulletin*, 54 (1999), 120-127.

16 Barber 1962, 45.

17 Barber 1962, 45.

18 Barber, "Wanderings in South Africa by Sea and Land, 1879", *Quarterly Bulletin of the South African Library*, Vol 17.3 (1963), 61.

19 Barber 1962, 43.

20 Barber 1962, 43.

21 Barber 1963, 67.

22 JJR Jolobe, "The Making of a Servant" in *Voices from Within: Black Poetry from Southern Africa*, Michael Chapman and Achmat Dangor (eds) (Johannesburg: Ad. Donker, 1982), 39-40.

23 Edward John Dunn, "Through Bushmanland" in *Selected Articles from the Cape Monthly Magazine 1870-76* (Cape Town: Van Riebeeck Society, 1978), 52-53.

24 Since this visit in 2003, the mine viewing platform and even the old mining museum itself have been supplanted by a new museum "experience", which is corporate in style and significantly more expensive than what I describe here.

25 Barber 1962, 51. In his article on Barber's interest in prehistory, Alan Cohen, (1999) makes this connection with Bishop Usher's dating of Creation at 4004.

26 Barber 1962, 42.

27 These names were recorded on different occasions and with different informants: BC 151, A2.1.8 (//Kabbo) May 1871: 288-291; BC 151, A1.4.25 (//Kabbo, ≠Kasin and /A!kunta) November 1873, 2341-2344; BC 151, A2.1.84 (/Han≠kass'o) May 1878, 6770-6775.

28 Research into primate ancestry is very accessibly presented in Janette and HJ Deacon's introduction to studies in the Stone Age, *Human Beginnings in South Africa: Uncovering the Secrets of the Stone Age* (Cape Town: David Philip, 1999).

My comments here, and on subsequent pages, draw in part on their discussion of primates, particularly of chimpanzees (42-47). For more about some of the ideological agendas involved in the discipline of primatology, see Donna Haraway's astute and engaging essay, "The Contest for Primate Nature: Daughters of Man-the-Hunter in the Field 1960-80" in *Simians, Cyborgs and Women: The Reinvention of Nature* (London: Free Association Books, 1991).

29 My UWC colleagues, Martin Legassick and Ciraj Rassool, have usefully examined this disgraceful period in the history of local museum collections in a book published jointly by the McGregor Museum and the South African Museum (now Iziko) under the evocative title, *Skeletons in the Cupboard: South African Museums and the Trade in Human Remains, 1907-1917* (Cape Town: South African Museum and McGregor Museum, Kimberley, 2000).

30 The McGregor Museum was informed of the skeletons at Gladstone at the end of April, 2003. In mid-May, the Prestwich bones were discovered in Cape Town. The questions mentioned here about ancestry and artefacts are from Nick Shepherd's "Archaeology Dreaming: Post-Apartheid Urban Imaginaries and the Bones of the Prestwich Street Dead" (*Journal of Social Archaeology*, 7.1 (2007), 21). This essay offers a very informative review of the "rival languages of concern" involved in the Prestwich story. He shows how in Cape Town there was outright conflict (polarised to a large extent along racial lines) between the interests expressed by the affected community and those of the archaeologists and heritage people who motivated for excavating the Prestwich site. While the activists claimed the human remains as ancestors, and argued for preserving the site intact to memorialise the presence of slaves and the poor in Cape Town society, the professionals defended the excavation in terms of the scientific information it would yield and as a means of "giving history back to the people". In spite of quite extensive public objections, the South African Heritage Resource Agency ruled that exhumation (and subsequent development of the site) should continue. Shepherd uses a narrative of this conflict to demonstrate limitations in the contemporary discipline of archaeology, and in the management of heritage resources, as currently practised in South Africa.

31 This comment is from the Abbé Henri Breuil. It is quoted in *Guide to Archaeological Sites in the Northern Cape* (Kimberley: McGregor Museum, 1990, 15), a detailed source of information and analysis compiled by Peter Beaumont and David Morris for the South African Association of Archaeologists' postconference excursion in 1990. This and their subsequent collection for another conference in 2004 (*Archaeology in the Northern Cape: Some Key Sites* (Kimberley: McGregor Museum, 2004)) have indeed been some of my key guides to the territory.

32 BC 151 A2.1.56, 4457-4525.

33 BC 151 A2.1.51, 4004-4009.

34 Wilhelm Bleek, "Bushman Researches. Parts 1 and 2", *Cape Monthly Magazine*, 11 (1875), 104-115; 150-155.

35 See, for example, Patricia Vinnicombe, *People of the Eland: Rock Paintings of the Drakensberg Bushmen as a Reflection of their Life and Thought* (Pietermaritzburg: University of Natal Press, 1976) and David Lewis-Williams, *Believing and Seeing: Symbolic Meaning in Southern San Rock Paintings* (London: Academic Press, 1981). A rich and growing corpus of work, including some quite intense debate, has been initiated by these studies.

36 In 2006 I received an email from David Morris with the sad news that Batista Salvador and his wife, Lolinda Dala, had both passed away.

37 This is discussed in more detail in David's unpublished MA thesis, *Driekopseiland and "The Rain's Magic Power": History and Landscape in a New Interpretation of a Northern Cape Rock Engraving Site* (University of the Western Cape, 2002), 135. My response in this chapter to Driekopseiland is strongly influenced by this impressive work.

38 David Morris uses Dia!kwain's phrase in the title of his thesis. He quotes as his source JD Lewis-Williams (ed), *Stories that Float from Afar: Ancestral Folklore of the San of Southern Africa* (Cape Town: David Philip, 2000), 273.

39 BC 151, A2.1.50, 3970-3974.

40 BC 151, A2.1.70, 5660-5664.

41 Andrew Bank considers in some detail the significance of homesickness and nostalgia in //Kabbo's poignant stories of home, and I am grateful to him for

drawing my attention to this aspect of the narratives. See "Narratives of Nostalgia, September 1872 and July 1873" in *Bushman in a Victorian World*, 197-202.

42 JM Coetzee, *White Writing: On the Culture of Letters in South Africa* (New Haven and London: Radix, 1988), 9.

43 On Kamfersdam, see Abe Abrahams and Mark D Anderson, "Messages from the Mud! Kamfers Dam, Waterbirds and Ramsar Status", in *African Wildlife*, 55.5 (2001), 20-21. For an example of Mark's research into flamingos in the region, see his article: "The Status of Flamingos in the Northern Cape Province, South Africa", *Ostrich*, 71 (2000), 431-434.

44 BP means "Before Present" in expressions of radiocarbon-dated ages, where "present" is defined as AD 1950. It was in that year that the Standard Reference sample for atmospheric ^{14}C was prepared for the calibration of radiocarbon measurements from ancient contexts. The term is now also used for dating methods other than radiocarbon.

45 BC 151 A2.1.70, 5698-5707.

46 See *Moffat of Kuruman* (London: The Sheldon Press, 1931), 3-4.

47 Moffat is quoted here in PHR Snyman, *Kuruman – vervloë pad na Afrika* (Pretoria: Raad vir Geesteswetenskaplike Navorsing, 1992), 7.

48 This point is made by Jacobs in *Environment, Power, and Injustice: A South African History* (New York: Cambridge University Press, 2003), 11.

49 This and other information about Afrikaner culture in Kuruman is from Snyman 1992, 169-71, 148-9.

50 Snyman 1992, 171.

51 Quoted in Snyman 1992, 7.

52 See V Twentyman-Jones, AJ Ribbink and D Voorvelt, "Colour Clues to Incipient Speciation of *Pseudocrenilabrus philander* (Teleostei, Cichlidae)", *South African Journal of Science*, Vol 93 November/December (1997), 534.

53 Jacobs 2003, 11-12.

54 Barbara Smuts, "Reflections" in JM Coetzee, *The Lives of Animals*, Amy Gutmann (ed.) (Princeton: Princeton University Press, 1999), 109-110.

55 Smuts, in Coetzee (1999), 118.

56 BC 151, A2.1.73, 5923v-5925v.

57 BC 151, A2.1.73, 5930-5947.

58 BC 151, A2.1.93, 7608-7625.

59 BC 151, A2.1.70, 5660.

60 BC 151, A2.1.21, 1453-1485.

61 Peter Beaumont, "Kathu Pan and Kathu Townlands / Uitkoms" in Morris and Beaumont's collection, *Archaeology in the Northern Cape: Some Key Sites* (2004), 52.

62 See Michael de Jongh's fascinating work in this field, in particular "Itinerant and Sedentary: Karretjie People, Agency and 'Karoo Culture'" (*South African Journal of Ethnography*, 23.1(2000), 1-13), and "No Fixed Abode: The Poorest of the Poor and Elusive Identities in Rural South Africa" (*Journal of Southern African Studies*, 28.2 (2002), 441-460).

63 He is quoted by David Morris in a discussion of the available literature in "Tsantsabane: The Blinkklipkop Specularite Mine, and Doornfontein", in Morris and Beaumont (2004), 54. David's account has been a valuable resource for this chapter.

64 J Campbell, *Journal of Travels in South Africa* (London: Religious Tract Society, 1835), 112.

65 Quoted by David Morris in "Tsantsabane" (2004), 55.

66 BC 151, A2.1.89, 7272v-7273v.

67 BC 151, A2.1.89, 7275v.

68 BC 151, A2.1.89, 7275-7280.

69 Once the Gladstone investigation was completed it became clear that the burials did in fact reflect a period of what he calls here "ordinary time" in the early days of Kimberley. In the end 15 of the 145 damaged graves at the Gladstone site were investigated, yielding just over 100 skeletons. Over the five months that this took, some of the team of previously unemployed people working at the site became very skilled excavators, and several have continued to be involved in aspects of archaeological work. Once the excavation was complete, a cleansing ceremony took place in the museum storeroom, with a group of sangomas burning herbs and chanting.

70 Since our conversations with Peter Beaumont about Wonderwerk Cave and Kathu Townlands, archaeologists Michael Chazan and Liora Horwitz obtained permits for their team to excavate Wonderwerk Cave and other sites in the region. Their preliminary findings at Wonderwerk suggest that the dating of hominin occupation of the cave may be even earlier than Peter Beaumont's work indicated. In a paper entitled "Radiometric Dating of the Earlier Stone Age Sequence in Excavation 1 at Wonderwerk Cave, South Africa: Preliminary Results" (in press, *Journal of Human Evolution*), the authors (Michael Chazan, Hagai Ron, Ari Matmon, Naomi Porat, Paul Goldberg, Royden Yates, Margaret Avery, Alexandra Sumner and Liora Kolska Horwitz) show that the onset of the Acheulean period at this site may have been as early as 1.6 million years ago, which is roughly contemporaneous with that of East Africa. The datings they have so far also suggest that the occupation of the cave during the Earlier Stone Age may have begun as far back as the Oldowan. Further excavation and analysis will help to elucidate things. But so far it appears that the Wonderwerk site may, as they put it, "represent the earliest evidence for intentional cave exploitation worldwide" (17). It remains to be seen whether their research will confirm Peter's hypothesis that the oldest ash layers at Wonderwerk are the result of human activity. As Michael Chazan put it in an email to me in early 2008, there is considerable evidence for burning in the front part of the site going back over 1.5 million years. But while the team has found stone tools that have been subjected to very high temperatures, and also some burnt animal bones, given the significance of this issue they are being extremely cautious about drawing conclusions at this stage of the investigation.

71 See Rita Covas, Charles R Brown, Mark D Anderson and Mary Bomberger Brown, "Stabilizing Selection on Body Mass in the Sociable Weaver *Philetarius socius*", *Proceedings of the Royal Society of London B*, 269, 1905-1909.

72 Barber 1963, 72.

ACKNOWLEDGMENTS

Very many people have contributed in different ways to making this book happen. I am grateful to you all. I would especially like to thank Duncan Miller for first telling me about Kathu and the other sites, for sharing with me his enthusiasm and his materials about the region, and for reading a draft of the manuscript. Once the journey began, many others also helped me think and write about it. Thank you in particular to the National Arts Council for the award of a Writer's Grant, the University of the Western Cape for funding my research costs, and my colleagues in the English Department for enabling me to take some time to write. Since our first meeting at the McGregor Museum, David Morris has continued to be an extraordinarily instructive, patient and generous guide to the territory, and has become a good friend in the process. Peter Beaumont was a fascinating and informative teacher, and at the Northern Cape sites we visited, Anthony Simpson and Neels Lehule and the late Batista Salvador warmly shared information, ideas and feelings. Mark Anderson sent me his research into sociable weavers and flamingos, Tania Anderson was very helpful about the botany of the region, and Michael Schoeman passed on the research about fish at Kuruman. Andrew Bank read several of the chapters with a very informed, attentive and sympathetic eye, and Janette Deacon was insightful and kind in sharing her work on the San. Among many conversations, both in person and via email, I especially remember the helpfulness of Jane Alexander, Michael Chazan, Liora Horwitz, Tony Humphreys, Ruth Kansky, Barry Lopez, John Parkington, Denis Raphaely, Nick Shepherd, Pippa Skotnes and Royden Yates. I am grateful to Zulfa Abrahams for tracking some references and to my friends Fiona Anderson and Kay McCormick for their insight and support. I have enjoyed working with the team at Kwela Books, and would particularly like to thank Elsa Silke for her careful editing of the text, and Nèlleke de Jager for her enthusiasm, thoughtfulness and precision throughout the publication process.

As always, my gratitude to Michael Cope is immense. Without his insight, love, companionship, practical help, attentive reading and constant encouragement, this book would really never have been written. His own book, *Ghaap: Sonnets from the Northern Cape* (Cape Town: Kwela Books/Snailpress, 2005), is a beautiful response to the same trip. I would also like to thank my mother, Elizabeth Martin, for her wisdom and generosity, and our twins, Sophie and Sky, who were part of the journey and who agreed to being written about.

Finally, this story is dedicated to Gary Snyder, with gratitude for his writings and for our long long-distance friendship.

JULIA MARTIN grew up in Pietermaritzburg and now lives in Muizenberg with her family. She has published a variety of poems, stories and essays, and has a special interest in ecology. She teaches in the English Department at the University of the Western Cape.